D1368658

LYONS
AND ITS REGION

TEXT
M.-H. CHAPLAIN
F. BAYARD

PHOTOGRAPHS
C. DELPAL
M. CARBONARE

TRANSLATION: ENTREPRISES 35

Éditions Ouest-France

Contents

Fourvière Hill

CHAPTER 1

Any visit to Lyons must begin with Fourvière Hill, as it is here that the city actually originated (Fourvière means 'Forum Vetus'), even though it is known today that other sites in the region had been occupied before the foundation of the colony here by Munatius Plancus, governor of the Three Gauls (Belgian Gaul, Celtic Gaul, and Aquitaine), for Roman citizens driven out of Vienne in 43 B.C. The roots of Christianity are also to be found on this site, as it was the first in Gaul to be converted to Christianity, and, indeed, its faith remains firm to this day, as on the 8th of December, the feast of the Immaculate Conception, the words 'Marie, mère de Dieu' (Mary, mother of God) are displayed across the hill. What is more, the large terrace at the side of the church is an excellent viewpoint from which to see the city spread out at the foot of the hill, then the area between the rivers Rhône and Sâone, and, finally, the plain of the Dauphiné. It is a sure sign of rain the next day if, in addition to all this, the Alps are also visible. A more extensive view in all directions is to be had from the observatory in the church's Saint-Michel tower, from where the more recently populated western part of the city can also be seen. In addition to the views, the three walks described here are especially attractive because of the open nature of this part of Lyons.

FOURVIÈRE

Fourvière can be reached on foot or by car up the many roads and paths that climb the slopes (montées). However, the most unusual and quickest way of getting to the top is by the funicular railway that leaves from the Gare Saint-Jean.

RELIGIOUS BUILDINGS

The sheer mass of the church, once described as 'an elephant upside-down on its back with its feet in the air', is overpowering when first seen from the square in front of it. Its construction was the result of two vows. In the 12th century, a small chapel dedicated to the Virgin Mary and St Thomas à Becket, the Archbishop of Canterbury murdered at the altar by Henry II's men, had been constructed on the deserted site of the old forum. In 1643, Lyons' city council, fearing the spread of the plague, dedicated the city to the Virgin Mary and resolved to walk up to the chapel every year if she spared it. Lyons was untouched by the plague, and so this has been done every 8th December, right up to the present day. The chapel was enlarged, and in 1852 received a new bell-tower, on top of which was placed a gilded statue of the Virgin of Fabisch. When this was inaugurated on 8th December, the people of Lyons quite spontaneously lit candles to decorate their windows, and this, so it is said, was the origin of the 8th of December illuminations. However, the local dignitaries who were members of the Fourvière Commission wanted to do even more, and the Franco-Prussian War of 1870 precipitated their decision. Archbishop de Ginoulhiac vowed to consecrate a new place of worship to the Virgin Mary if the Prussians did not invade Lyons, which they did not. The church's construction was financed by the opening of a special fund, and the first stone was laid in 1872. Pierre Bossan, the architect, was heavily influenced both by the Norman architecture of Sicily and by symbolism,

Opposite:
Fourvière Hill, the original site of the city, overlooks the Saint-Jean district and the cathedral.

Inside the church, the gold of the mosaics glorifies the worship of the period.

and conceived the path of Christians through the church as a rite of initiation. Bossan, however, died in 1888, and Sainte-Marie Perrin took charge of the building, which was completed in 1896. The interior decoration, which was started at the same time, has still not been completed.

The church looks like a fortress as it has four towers complete with battlements which rise to a height of 48.5 metres, and which symbolise Justice and Strength (to the west), and Prudence and Temperance (to the east). The main portico has three high arches carved with evangelical symbols, above

Lyons' 'montées'

Eight 'montées' (ascents or ways up) can be followed to get to Fourvière. But be warned ! Many of them are simply staircases. The Montée des Epies (formerly called Des Pyes), which has a terraced garden, starts in front of the church of Saint-Georges. The attractive Montée du Gourguillon begins in the Place de la Trinité, whilst the Protestants built the Montée du Chemin Neuf leading from the Place Saint-Jean in 1562. The Jardins du Rosaire (Rosary Gardens), which line the hillside from Notre-Dame-de-Fourvière, border this latter 'montée'. Between Saint-Jean and Saint-Paul are situated the Montée des Chazeaux (or Tire-Cul), the Montée du Garillan, the Montée du Change, the Ruelle Punaise, the Montée des Carmes-Déchaussés (238 steps), and the Montée Nicolas-de-Lange (560 steps). All have their own particular charm, and enable the city to be seen from high up, and so from a completely different perspective. If going up the 'montées' is too much like hard work, they can always be used for going back down.

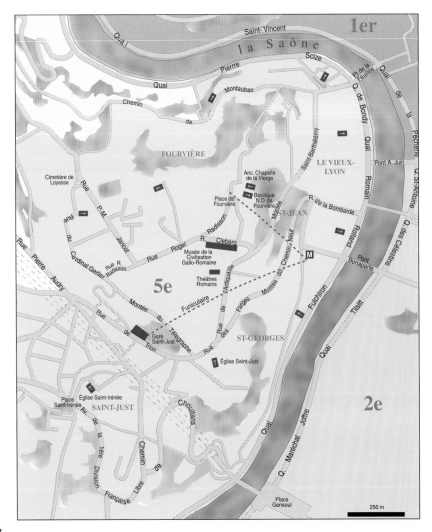

which is a gallery whose openings are supported by pillars in the form of draped angelic figures. In the centre of a triangular pediment by Charles Dufraine stands the Virgin Mary in majesty with the Infant Jesus, with the archangel Gabriel, the healer, and the city councillors' vow of 1643 to the right, and the archangel St Michael, the fighter, with the vow of 1870, the archbishops who promoted the construction, and an angel driving back the invasion on the left. Further along the square in front of the church is the entrance to the crypt which serves as the church's platform, and which is guarded by the Lion of Judah, by Charles Dufraine. The church porch stands at the top of some steps, and on its back wall, between Adam and Eve and Cain and Abel, the families of soldiers killed in 1940 have placed a frieze by Belloni depicting Lyons' saints. The bronze entrance doors are decorated with angels supporting, on the right, Noah's Ark, and, on the left, the Ark of the Covenant. The side walls of the church's exterior are also carved. On the north wall are depicted the theological virtues of faith, hope, and charity, represented by women from the Old Testament and biblical vegetation, while the south wall is dedicated to chastity, but has not been completed. The double-galleried chevet lies on top of the Porte des Lions (Lions Gate), which is half-hidden by the vegetation on the hillside and which is rarely used.

Whether the church is entered either by the crypt dedicated to St Joseph, as was Bossini's intention as he wanted to show that the earthly life of Mary and Jesus has been supported by Joseph's work, or by the upper doorway, the wealth of decoration and the brilliance of its colours is stunning, with blue, the Virgin Mary's colour, and gold being dominant, and with everything being beautifully set off by the simplicity of the church's design. Sculptures and mosaics by Charles Lemeire and, from 1911, Georges Décote, as well as the latter's stained glass windows, are an important part of the internal decoration, their themes being expressions of the subjects of religious devotion of the period, the doctrines of the Immaculate Conception and papal infallibility, and the worship of Joan of Arc. It is, however, the Virgin Mary who is most glorified for her earthly (side-altar sculptures) and heavenly (stained glass windows in the nave depicting Mary's sovereignty) personae, in addition to her importance both in the history of the Roman Catholic Church (mosaics on the north wall) and that of France (mosaics on the south wall). The church's roof is made up of several domes. The Virgin Mary appears on three of the central bays as daughter of the Father, wife of the Spirit, and mother of the Son. Her statue on the high altar overlooks the Pavement of the Heresies, which are represented by verses that recall the condemnations of the Syllabus published by Pope Pious IX in 1864, which summarised what were, in his opinion, the main 'errors' of the modern world. These included liberalism, socialism, and naturalism. The church has only one painting (on the back of the main façade), which was executed by Ordel at the time of the cholera epidemic in 1832, and completed by his pupil, Tyr, in 1852.

In contrast to all this, the original chapel (to the right of the church) was enlarged in 1681, and decorated with an altar and an altarpiece ornamented with angels by Delamonce in 1739. However, pilgrims come here to see the comparatively modest 16th century Black Virgin. In the same direction, the Musée de l'Oeuvre has displays of vestments and other objects used in church worship, as well as a superb collection of 'ex votos', which either ask the Virgin Mary for her

The sculptured side walls.

The statue of the Virgin Mary by Fabisch.

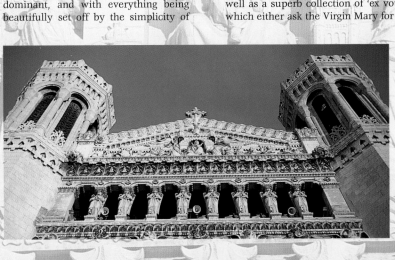

The main front of the church has a portico of three lofty arcades, a gallery, and a triangular pediment.

The Metallic Tower is a television relay station.

Superb views over the city can be enjoyed from the Quatre-Vents footbridge in the Parc des Hauteurs.

help or thank her for having given it. A beautiful neo-Classical gateway by Pollet (1831) gives access to the Fourvière restaurant, which has views of Lyon spreading out at its feet.

PARC DES HAUTEURS

Once back on the church square, turn left, passing in front of the bishop's palace and the area that has been recently laid-out for reception of the annual pilgrimage. The Tour Métallique (Metallic Tower) is 86 metres high, and was built in 1894 by a Monsieur Gay to act as a 'Republican lighthouse' during the Lyons world exhibition. The tower used to have a restaurant with panoramic views, but it is used today as a television transmitter. On the left, you can go into the Parc des Hauteurs and follow the Passerelle des Quatre-Vents that was built in 1993 on the track of the tramlines which used to be an extension of the funicular railway from Saint-Paul to Fourvière and the Loyasse cemetery. This walk provides good views of the Saône and the hill of Croix-Rousse with the Charterhouse of St Bruno. At the end of the path can be seen the staring point of the old Sarra arti-

The Loyasse cemetery was developed between 1807 and 1810, and still has many of its first tombstones.

ficial ski slope, which is now sometimes used for mountain biking competitions, and then the Loyasse cemetery.

On leaving the cemetery, continue along Rue du Cardinal Gerlier, then turn left along the Rue Roger Radisson which follows the route of the Roman Aquitaine Way. At number 23, the garden of the Visitation, an old 19th century convent which is now used as the record office for civil (i.e. non-religious) hospices, can be visited. There is also a adjoining cloister with some deconsecrated prefabricated buildings.

ARCHAEOLOGICAL MUSEUM AND PARK

The Musée de la Civilisation Gallo-Romaine (Museum of Roman Civilisation), designed by Bernard Zehrfuss, was built of shuttered concrete in 1976 and lies practically buried in the hillside at the corner of Rue Radisson and Rue Cléberg. Within the museum, arranged along a 320-metre slope, are seventeen exhibition rooms which are mainly devoted to displays of daily life in Lyons during the Roman period. In two places, a mosaic in the room below can be seen through openings in the floor. A visit to the museum promotes a much better understanding of Lyons' Roman remains, and especially as to how the theatres operated.Entrance to the archaeological park is either from the top (17, rue Cléberg) or from the bottom (6, rue Antiquaille). The first official excavations were carried out in 1933 on the site where trial digs had taken place in the late 19th and early 20th centuries in order to find the amphitheatre where the first Christians had been tortured to death in 177. These excavations have continued ever since, without any interruption, bringing streets, shops, and three buildings to light. The 1st century theatre is 108.5 metres in diameter, and could accommodate 10,500 people on its three series of tiered seating, which was originally covered in white stone. All this rested on a system of arched galleries which were supported by radiating walls and other surrounding concentric structures. The orchestra floor is a reconstruction, as are the four tiers of seating for senators. The 46 metres long and 3.8 metres wide pit where the curtain that used to signal the beginning and end of a performance used to be fixed, has been preserved, but is hidden under the floor that covers the hyposcaenium, or under stage area, whose mechanism can be seen in the museum. Of the stage wall, there remain only the foundations, whilst a three-

One of the Musée de la Civilisation Gallo-Romaine's 17 rooms.

The Claudian tablets contain a speech by the Emperor Claudius.

The theatre could accommodate 10,500 people on three levels of tiered seating.

columned portico extends out in front of the theatre. To the south, after an open space, is the 2nd century Odeon, which is identical in plan, but, at 73 metres, smaller in diameter. Such a monument is fairly rare, as only twenty have been discovered in the Roman world, and was reserved for orations and concerts. It is thought that it was roofed over, although no trace of this exists. Nowadays, the Odeon, together with the theatre, is the setting for performances each summer during the Fourvière festival. A monumental construction uncovered above the theatre was, for a long time, thought to have been the Temple of Cybele, whose worship is known to have been very popular in Lyons, as a head of the goddess and three altars used for the sacrifice of bulls, an essential part of the goddess' worship, have been unearthed. However, the experts today are questioning this identification of the temple and the statue, as there were several successive occupations of the site between 40 B.C. and 10 A.D., one of which would correspond to the palace of the Emperor Agrippa.

On leaving the archaeological park, take the Rue de l'Antiquaille, where, at number 1, the old 17th century Visitandine convent can be visited. It was converted into a hospital in the 19th century, and contains 'St Pothin's crypt', which was decorated with mosaics during the 19th century. It is said that the adjoining recess was used as a hiding place by St Pothin, the first bishop of Lyons, in 177. When leaving, turn left along the same street.

SAINT-JUST

The Saint-Just-Sainte-Irénée district of Lyons developed over an extensive burial ground on the edge of the Aquitaine and Narbonne Ways on the way to Roanne. Two churches were built here in the 5th century, and around them grew up a powerful religious community of twelve and later thirty-five canons in the

Loyasse cemetery

Burials in churchyards have been forbidden in France since 1776, and cemeteries have had to be moved away from buildings. Since 1804, burials have also had to be individual. To ensure the application of these laws, the City of Lyons bought several pieces of land in the Loyasse area between 1807 and 1810, and entrusted the works to the architect, Joseph Gay. The first burials took place in 1808, and very soon some beautiful monuments first appeared along the paths laid out for them at the bottom of the cemetery (81, 79, 59, 61, 7, 9, 1, 2, 4), and then everywhere else, the space reserved for ordinary burials decreasing accordingly. As the burial plots are granted in perpetuity, the funereal monuments have remained, and so an excellent lesson in funerary art can be had today by walking around them. Until the early 20th century, the tombs had to have railings around them, but that is not the case now.
The monuments are either made up of recumbent stones (slabs or sarcophagi), upright stones (columns, obelisks, pyramids, towers, crosses, and gravestones), or a combination of these types. Some have a flat wall at the back whilst others have a central projecting part. Some of them are real covered buildings (chapels, neo-Greek and neo-Egyptian temples, funerary niches, and canopies), while others have statues depicting the deceased person, and which are set off by the accompanying architectural composition. In the case of family tombs, the burial plot contains gravestones bearing the names of several people, or a central cross, or a back wall. A taste for classical styles of architecture was a great influence on the first tombs, and this was followed by the appearance of the neo-Gothic style together with Christian symbols, and metal and stained glass was used in addition to stone. During the 20th century, the tombs have become simpler and more uniform in style.

11

The Maccabees, St Irenée, and St Just

The Maccabees were seven Jewish brothers who were executed in Palestine by Antiochus IV, the king of Syria, in the 2nd century B.C. because they rebelled against him in defence of their religion. They became symbolic figures for the Christian martyrs, and it is said that their relics had been moved to the church of St Peter in Vinculi in Rome, from where their worship spread out to the first Christian communities.

Irenée, who was taught by St Polycarp, the bishop of Smyrna, and also a disciple of the apostle, John, became the second bishop of Lyons, and the author of an important book on theology.

St Just was the 13th bishop of Lyons. He felt personally responsible for the lynching by the mob of some sort of maniac who had taken refuge in his cathedral, and so resigned his post, and retired to a monastery in Egypt, where he died in about 400. The people of Lyons went there to fetch his body back to the city, and buried it in a mausoleum and then in the church of the Macchabées.

9th century. This became a separate town with its own walls in the 14th century, but was later brought back under the jurisdiction of Lyons in 1562 following the destruction of the walls by the Protestants. Changes made to the district during the 1970s saw the disappearance of many old houses, but led to the discovery of Roman buildings.

Go through the Place des Minimes, which was the name of a monastery suppressed in 1791, and past the 19th century 'lycée' (secondary school) of the same name. Opposite stands the Lycée de Saint-Just, whose buildings were formerly those of a large seminary erected in the 19th century by Tony Desjardins. Lower down, underneath a courtyard, is an underground Roman reservoir, the Bérelle cave, which measures 230 m^3, was listed as an historical monument in 1862, but which receives very few visitors.

In the Rue des Farges, stop at number 6, where the site of some Roman houses dating from the late 1st century B.C., but abandoned in the 2nd century A.D., was discovered during the construction of this modern building. It was here that the importance of earthen construction in domestic Roman architecture was noted. Part of the uncovered remains, in particular the former baths, can be seen behind the blocks of flats. At number 43 stands the church dedicated to the Maccabees and St Just. It was built in 1590 and enlarged in 1661, with the Jesuit façade designed by Delamonce being added in 1711. Statues of St Just

The traces of three successive churches dedicated to St Just are marked out by different-coloured blocks.

and St Irénée stand on either side of the front. Above the side doors are two 1828 bas-reliefs by Legendre-Héral which depict the worship of the relics of St Just and the martyrdom of St Irénée. Inside, there is a triumphal arch in the form of a canopy and some paintings in the sacristy. The present church replaced an older one that was destroyed by the Protestants in 1562, and of which some remains can be seen in the Rue des Macchabées.

Along the route, stop at the Place de l'Abbé Larue, with its orientation table and benches, to enjoy the extensive view of Lyons, then turn immediately into the Rue de Trion, where a 19th century fountain can be seen at number 8, and then turn left into the Rue des Macchabées. A wall painting between numbers 9 and 11 is a reproduction of part of a 1550 plan of the city that depicts the church before its destruction, while at ground level, the outlines of three successive churches dedicated to St Just have been marked out in different colours. From the 4th century onwards, a religious community served the church of the burial ground that was dedicated to the Maccabees. This first church was rebuilt in the late 5th and early 6th centuries in order to house the body of St Just, was restored in the 9th century, and completely rebuilt during the 12th and 13th centuries. It had three naves, a semi-circular apse, and two towers rising above each end of the transept. The 16th century Bellièvre tower can be seen, through a glass door, at number 19 ter, as well as, at number 19, the Taurobole (bull sacrifice) Fountain and its Doric portico, designed by Louis Flacheron in 1828.

Before going back to Saint-Irénée, turn left at the end of the Rue des Macchabées to go up the Montée des Choulans as far as the Place Wernert, where there are five large Roman mausoleums, discovered, among other remains, in 1885, during excavations carried out at the time of the construction of the railway station in west Lyons. As they were thought to be extremely beautiful, despite the fact that their upper levels were missing, they were dismantled stone by stone and transported and reassembled here. In the middle is the one that five freed slaves offered to Quintus Calvius Turpio, whereas that of Satrius is the largest. The three others are those of Julia, which has a false door carved on it, Quintus Valerius, and Julius Severianus. Some funeral urns, a sarcophagus, and other remains are displayed around them. Go back to the Rue des Macchabées and to the church of Saint-Irénée.

The church of Saint-Irénée was rebuilt by Flacheron and Benoît between 1820 and 1830.

SAINT-IRÉNÉE

This church was built in the 5th century on the burial ground where two of the martyrs of 177 had been buried, and a trace of one of its entrances is still visible in the north wall of the present church. However, the church has experienced many trials and tribulations. It was rebuilt and restored in the 9th century, and later rebuilt in the Romanesque style in the 12th century, but only the crypt remains of this church, as it was destroyed by the Protestants in 1562. After several attempts at repairing it, it was finally replaced by the present neo-Baroque style church, designed by Flacheron and Benoît, during the period 1824 to 1830. Inside the upper church can be seen the remains of a 12th century mosaic depicting the signs of the zodiac, the months, the arts, and the theological virtues of faith, hope, and charity, whilst the 19th century stained glass windows, including some by Lucien Bégule, depict scenes from the early Church in Lyons. The crypt was renovated by Tony Desjardins in 1863, and in it have been collected some early Christian funerary inscriptions as well as altars which would have been the martyrs' tombs.

Some sarcophagi have been laid out in the churchyard, where, behind the chevet, there is a calvary monument, which marked the destination of one of the city's Ways of the Cross, which left from the church of Sainte-Croix. There is evidence of its existence in 1687, but it was destroyed in 1793, and then restored in 1814 and 1868. It is made up of the three crosses of Christ and the two thieves, twelve niches, and an underground chapel, which is closed to the public, that houses a sculpture of Christ in the tomb, and which formed the fourteenth station of the cross.

Saint-Irénée's fort, constructed between 1831 and 1841, can be seen opposite the church. From 1921 to 1946, it accommodated 473 Chinese students who had come to Lyons to study at the university, a fact which is revealed by an inscription over the gateway. Today it is used as a university hall of residence as well as housing the Ecole Nationale Supérieure des Arts et Techniques du Théâtre (a university level drama school). Not far up the Rue du Commandant Charcot, there is a series of arches and a pillar which used to support the reservoir for one of the Gier aqueduct's four siphons during Roman times.

In the Montée des Génovéfains, a terraced garden with a view of the front of the Maison des Génovéfains can be seen at number 1. The house was built in 1740 by Loyer to the plans of Soufflot, and was paid for by the son of Philippe, duke of Orleans, the former Regent of France. Today it is the headquarters of the Lyons diocese, as well as housing several other organisations, including Radio Fourvière.

Go down the Montée de Choulans to the district of Quarantaine. There are superb views of the city all along the route.

The 18th century façade of the church dedicated to the Maccabees and St Just.

O l d   L y o n s

CHAPTER 2

Old Lyons is most certainly the most famous part of the capital of the three Gauls. It was the first area in France to be restored under the initiative of André Malraux (Minister of Culture, 1959-1969), and played an extremely important part in getting the city listed as a UNESCO world heritage site. Two walks setting off from the Place Saint-Jean are recommended here.

FROM SAINT-JEAN TO SAINT-PAUL

The northern part of Old Lyons is the most famous. It is also the most beautiful because here, in medieval times, lived the clergymen, judges, merchants, and foreign bankers who attracted Lyons' four annual fairs from the late 15th century onwards. However, until 1962 and the law concerning the restoration of old, historic urban areas, the buildings, which had hardly changed at all since their construction between the 15th and 17th centuries, were in a similar dilapidated state to those of the textile-workers' homes in Saint-Georges. Restoration work in the area has now been completely finished.

The area can be divided into two easily distinguishable parts since the construction of the Saint-Paul station has divided what used to be a single unit.

SAINT-JEAN

This area is divided into four parts that are each identifiable by their own particular landmarks, but through them all, however, ran what was the city's main residential area until the mid-17th century. Strolling along and going into a courtyard to admire the backs of the buildings, which are often more beautiful than the street frontages as no-one in Lyons liked to make too much of an outward show of their wealth, is what makes this such an attractive district. It does, however, help to know what to look out for. The late medieval houses in Lyons are very distinctive. In those days

The construction of the Cathedral of Saint-Jean-Baptiste took 600 years to complete.

The winding Rue Saint-Jean.

Opposite:
At 19, rue du Boeuf, the Maison de l'Outarde d'Or (House of the Golden Bustard) displays all the architectural features that are so characteristic of the area.

15

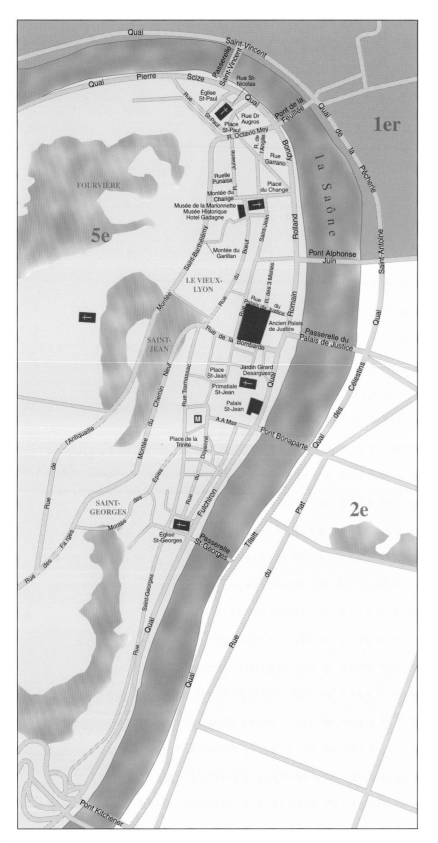

(just like today, since this is now a pedestrian area), all traffic was foot traffic, as there was no space provided for horses or coaches. When coaches became an indispensable and pretentious display of wealth and luxury, the rich people who used them moved away from Saint-Jean to live in Bellecour and Ainay.

In addition to Saint-Jean's most famous historical monuments, all the facades, all the doorways, all the alleys, all the courtyards, all the towers, all the galleries, and all the 'traboules' (passages connecting one street with another) deserve be mentioned. However, choices have had to be made, and so only the most noteworthy have been selected.

CATHEDRAL OF SAINT-JEAN AND ITS CLOSE

On entering the Place Saint-Jean, which was redeveloped in the 19th century, the view of the cathedral of Saint-Jean-Baptiste is striking. Housing the holy relic of the saint's jawbone which was given to the cathedral by the Duc de Berry, the cathedral is 79 metres long, 13.3 metres long, and 32.5 metres high at its highest vault. More than its size, however, it is its massiveness that holds the attention, as its towers are uncompleted and therefore not very high at 44 metres – not exactly raising it heavenward. In many cities, three churches were built side by side for the purposes of worship, that for the bishop, that for the faithful, and that for baptisms. The cathedral of Saint-Jean is the sole remaining building of such a group of cathedral buildings, which also comprised the churches of Saint-Etienne and Sainte-Croix, whose remains can now be seen in the Girard-Desargues archaeological park to the left of the cathedral. They were uncovered in the late 1960s following the demolition of some dilapidated houses.

ARCHAEOLOGICAL PARK

The baptistery of Saint-Etienne, formed of an octagonal basin standing in the centre of a rectangular room with an apse and apsidal chapels, was in use from the 4th century. It was made into a church in the 9th century, was changed into the shape of a Greek cross during the Romanesque period, but was destroyed during the Revolution. Nothing remains of the church of Sainte-Croix,

A Gothic arch, together with the apse's Romanesque foundations, is all that remains of the church of Sainte-Croix, which was demolished in the 19th century.

The market in the Place Saint-Jean, in the middle of which is the 19th century fountain depicting the baptism of Christ.

which was demolished in the 19th century, except for the Romanesque foundations of the apse and a Gothic arch.

The present cathedral is not the first church to have been built on this site, as, with the permission of the priest at 70, rue Saint-Jean, a crypt, under the choir of Saint-Jean, can be seen. This contains the remains of a 4th century apse and of a mosaic floor that was uncovered in 1935, as well as evidence of changes to the building carried out between the 5th and 12th centuries.

CATHEDRAL OF SAINT-JEAN

The present building is a result of the determination of Archbishop Guichard (1181–1193), who started the construction of the Romanesque church, which, however, took several centuries to complete. His successor, Jean de Bellemains (1181–1193) continued the work on the choir, and Archbishop Renaud (1193–1226) had the transept, the eastern part of the nave, and the foundations of the west bay built. The nave was constructed during the 13th century, as and when money was found to finance the work. The west bay, the west front, and the chevet's north tower date from the 14th century, while the side chapels were built between the 15th and 17th centuries. The construction work was plagued with problems all the way through. In about 1230, because of the

fact that the construction was not on solid ground, the stonework cracked, as, for example, in the triforium in the choir and the transept crossing, and the chevet tipped southwards. As the continuation of worship had to be ensured, the new church was built to fit tightly round the old, thereby complicating the work considerably, and restoration work was necessary in the 15th century. In 1562, iconoclastic Protestants smashed up the statues of the saints on the west front, and in 1756, the medieval doors were replaced, for some reason to do with worship, by those, designed by de Soufflot's studio, which stand there today. The destruction of the city's bridges in 1944 also caused some damage to the structure.

The west front can be better appreciated from the centre of the square, near the 19th century fountain depicting Christ's baptism. The central doorway and the two side doorways with their carved archivolts are crowned with Gothic gables, whilst above this is a series of blind arcading finishing with a balustrade forms the first floor. It bears the carved coats-of-arms of the Pope and of the king of France. The second part of the west front is made up of a wall with a rose window in its centre, and decorated on the left by a clock that dates from 1394, and on the right by two empty niches supported by carved brackets. On the third floor, between the two towers, a triangular gable is pierced by a Gothic

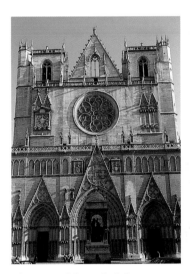

The towers of the Cathedral of Saint-Jean-Baptiste remain uncompleted.

Astronomical clock in the cathedral of Saint-Jean

The clock strikes at 12 noon, 2pm, and 3pm, when the automated figures spring into action. A cock flaps its wings, some musical angels blow their trumpets, and the angel Gabriel appears to the Virgin Mary, upon whom the Holy Spirit descends in the form of a dove. God blesses the scene, and a Swiss guard goes round the upper gallery. The astrolabe with the moon, the sun, and the 24 hourly numbers is underneath the clock.

The 19th century astronomical clock.

*Like many houses in Lyons,
the Hôtel Paterin has a
statuette of the Virgin Mary
standing in a niche.*

24, rue Saint-Jean

opening which is framed by statues of the Virgin Mary and the archangel Gabriel, finished off with a statue of God.

The most precious features on the west front must be examined close to. These are the 320 early 14th century medallions that are carved below the recessed arches of the archivolt, and that should be read from the bottom and from the outside. They represent a very varied range of subjects, both sacred and profane, including those of work throughout the months, signs of the zodiac, scenes from the lives of St John the Baptist, St Peter, and Christ, saints, animals, and scenes from everyday life. It brings to mind those of the Portail des Libraires (Booksellers' Doorway) in Rouen Cathedral.

Inside, the building's size and evolution can best be appreciated in the choir. The plan is simple, comprising a central nave, two side aisles, side chapels in the walls, a transept, and a semi-circular apse. The choir is Romanesque, the Gothic architecture beginning in the transept and changing in style towards the end of the nave. The cathedral has a classic elevation of large arcades, a triforium, and then high windows. Sexpartite vaulting is not so common as quadripartite vaulting is normally predominant, this being supported by external buttresses. The most interesting decoration is in the choir, where red and brown inlaid work makes up a frieze that is Italian in inspiration, and where also the ornate capitals of the upper columns indicate a Byzantine influence in the carvings of the three kings on horseback, Christ, the Virgin Mary with the Christ

Child, and the Christ Child's bath, as well as an influence from Vienne in the depiction of grimacing masks. The furnishings are far from extravagant, with two 18th century sculptures of St Stephen and St John the Baptist facing each other across the nave, a 16th century astronomical clock that has been repaired countless times, a 19th century organ, and a great many paintings, most of which came from the collections of Cardinal Fesch, archbishop of Lyons and Napoleon Bonaparte's uncle, and which used to hang in Paris churches. The great 13th century stained glass windows in the apse recall the history of the Church in Lyons, its patron saints, and the core concepts of Christianity. The two rose windows in the transept, which also date from the 13th century, depict, to the north, Christ surrounded by good and evil angels, and, to the south, Adam and Eve with scenes from the life of Christ. The 14th century rose window in the west front portrays the lives of St John the Baptist and St Stephen.

The final chapel in the southern side aisle was built in the Flamboyant Gothic style in the 15th century in order to house the tomb, destroyed in 1562, of Cardinal Archbishop Charles de Bourbon. The vaulted ceiling has a wealth of ribs and pendant keystones, and the arches are decorated with vine-leaves and bunches of grapes. The name 'Charles' appears on a balustrade, and elsewhere can be seen not only his initials, but also those of his nephews and nieces. A stag holds a banderole that carries the inscription 'Espérance' (Hope).

MANÉCANTERIE (CHOIR SCHOOL)

This building stands to the right of the cathedral. It dates from the 11th century, and was, at first, the canons' refectory, but 200 years later became a song school for the priests, hence the name derived from the Latin 'mane cantare' (to sing in the morning). Its façade is somewhat austere with blind arcading resting on small capital-decorated columns, together with decorative red brickwork. Since its construction, it has undergone some alterations, with some openings being made and an extra floor being added.

ARCHBISHOP'S PALACE

The archbishop's residence and office were adjacent to the cathedral until 1906, but the palace's appearance has changed a lot since its foundation in the 6th century. Two square towers, the entrance arch of a chapel, and a staircase turret are medieval in date, but the palace is essentially a construction of the 18th and 19th centuries, the period when the Avenue Adolphe-Max was driven through, destroying in the process the 15th century gallery on the waterside. It is now called the Palais Saint-Jean, and forms an attractive group of buildings around a garden, together with the new Manécanterie, recently restored in yellow and blue, to the left, and to the

*The Rue Saint-Jean
is the area's main thoroughfare.*

right, the archbishop's palace itself, which now belongs to the City of Lyons, and which contains the City Record Office (which will soon be leaving), a branch library, and the Académie (education authority). The handsome porticoes on Doric columns are the work of Soufflot, who also designed the front of the building.

SAINT-JEAN'S WALLS

Throughout the Middle Ages, the Saint-Jean district was enclosed by a wall, which did not really disappear until the 19th century. Two segments of the wall remain under the Maison de Quartier (community centre) opposite the cathedral and the Demeure du Concierge (Concierge's House), so-called because the concierge had to close six gates, that was built by François d'Estaing between 1496 and 1516 near the Porte Froc, 37, rue Saint-Jean. This house is Flamboyant Gothic in style, as shown by its pilaster-framed windows and its tower, and there is a wall-plaque to say that the Marquise de Sévigné stayed there in 1672 and 1673. The house now belongs to the City of Lyons, which has plans to restore it and make it into a visitor centre.

THE JUSTICE AREA

The Rue de la Bombarde takes its name not from the 18th century bas-relief at number 10, but from the sign of a music school where the playing of the 'bombardon', or double bass, was taught. Cross the Rue de la Bombarde and continue along the Rue Saint-Jean, which is the area's main street, to the Justice district. The eyes are inevitably drawn to the courtyard of the Maison des Avocats (Law Society House) on the left and the back of the Palais de Justice (Law Courts) on the right.

The old inn of the Croix d'Or (Golden Cross), which was reconstructed during the Renaissance, used to accommodate lots of travellers, which explains its large size. Just like today's students at the Centre Régional de Formation de Jeunes Avocats (Regional Training Centre for Young Lawyers), they used to enter by the carriage entrance at 60, rue Saint-Jean. Before going to see the main front of the Palais de Justice, note the winding nature of the street and the attractive row of mullioned windows in the houses from numbers 54 to 40, as well as going into number 58's courtyard, where part of the stencilled frieze that has been

Tall, narrow buildings that extend a long way back from the street line the length of the Rue Saint-Jean.

The Maison des Avocats courtyard.

Musée de Gadagne excavations

The alteration works carried out at the Musée de Gadagne, especially with regard to the creation of two rooms at basement level, and two series of systematic excavations have led to a large number of discoveries which have shed light on the buildings and daily life in times gone by. A capital, some pieces of mullioned windows, and an icebox buried in the soil are evidence of quite a rich 14th to 15th century building, and has shed new light on the little known history of the Hôtel Gadagne. A 3rd and 4th century Roman hypocaust has called into question the Roman settlement in the Lyons area, as it now looks likely that the inhabitants of the Fourvière district came down the hill to settle there earlier than had been thought.

The Maison Thomassin at 2, place du Change is one of the oldest houses in the area.

found on the second floor of the house behind can be seen.

The Palais de Justice was built by Baltard between 1835 and 1845, and its main entrance is on the Quai Romain Rolland. The Palais de Roanne used to be the seat of the old seneschal's court during the 17th and 18th century, but nothing of this remains now but two painted ceilings by Thomas Blanchet. The building that succeeded it is a sort of temple with 24 columns, which have given it its popular name. An impressive staircase leads up to the colonnaded peristyle, which is decorated with Classical Roman emblems such as caissons (ammunition wagons), fasces of lictors, (a bundle of rods with a projecting axe-blade, carried by a lictor (magistrate's

officer) as a symbol of a magistrate's power), flowerets, Greek fret patterns, and spirals. The enormous Salle de Pas Perdus is decorated with allegorical bas-reliefs, such as 'The city of Lyons welcoming business' and 'The Arts' (1847), and 'Justice punishing crime' (1862), as well as having a three-domed ceiling depicting the signs of the zodiac. This is the place where Klaus Barbie was tried in 1987, but since the opening of new law courts at La Part-Dieu in 1995, only the 'cour d'appel' (Court of Appeal) and the 'cours d'assises' (Crown Court) continue to sit here.

If returning by the Rue du Palais du Justice, it would be a good idea to turn right into the Rue des Trois-Maries, which is a reminder of an inn sign representing Marie-Salomé, Marie-Jacobé, and Marie-Madeleine (Mary Magdalene). The front of the house at number 3 has a staircase, and number 15 still bears marks made by building labourers as well as lines used in the assembly of stones that had been prepared in advance. In the Place de la Baleine is situated the headquarters of the 'Renaissance du Vieux Lyon' organisation, which keeps a close eye on the area's preservation and restoration. Rejoining the Rue Saint-Jean, and going back a little way, the Maison des Le Visite can be seen at number 29. This is also called the 'Maison aux Pommes de Pin' as the small and slender columns that frame its windows rest on carvings of fir/pine cones. At number 27 is a 17th century house built of dressed and fluted stone, while at number 24, the Maison des Laurencin's courtyard reveals double strutted windows, an octagonal tower, and a 'traboule' towards the Rue du Boeuf.

THE GOUVERNEMENT AREA

The Place du Gouvernement owes its name to the fact that it used to be the site of the residence of the governors of the Lyonnais (the Lyons region), Beaujolais, and Forez, which was demolished in the 19th century. The governors were always members of the same family, the Neuville-Villeroys, and moved away when they decided that they preferred to live in a much larger house on the Presqu'île. Still to be found there today are a beautiful 17th century house at number 5, and, at number 2, the front of an old inn bearing the signs (sirens and dragons) of the prophylactic virtues. The opening of the basket-handled door gives access to a loggia, and then an upper courtyard, from where a 'traboule' leads to 10, quai Romain Rolland.

A Flamboyant Gothic facade in Saint-Jean.

Further along the Rue Saint-Jean, houses with Flamboyant Gothic-style fronts and courtyards at numbers 7, 9, and 11 can be seen. The house at number 11 belonged to the Scève family, whose son, Maurice, the humanist and poet, organised the royal visit to Lyons in 1548.

THE BUSINESS AREA

The Place du Change symbolises the business and banking activity which in the Middle Ages and early modern period brought life to the area during Lyons' great fairs. Merchants used to gather here in the open air, throughout the 16th century, in order to decide the exchange rates and lending rates from one fair to another. The first Loge du Change (exchange lodge) was built in 1653, and this was enlarged in 1750 by Jean-Baptiste Roche to designs by Soufflot, who gave it arches separated by rectangular Doric columns, and a floor with Ionic columns. After the Loge became a Protestant church in 1803, doors were fitted in 1854, and changes made to the interior. For the year 2000, a second clock has been put up to the left of the attic storey to match that on the right.

At number 2 is the Maison Thomassin, one of the oldest houses in Lyons, which was rebuilt in 1298, altered in the late 15th century, and enlarged to go down to the Quai Romain Rolland in the 17th century. The lattice windows topped with trefoil arches recall the cathedral's Gothic arches, and there is also a carved frieze of animals. The three coats of arms are those of the Dauphin, Charles VIII and

The Loge du Change was rebuilt in the 18th century to plans by Soufflot, before receiving its second clock in the year 2000.

Anne of Brittany. Work carried out in the house's interior has revealed a ceiling painted with the coats of arms of St Louis and Blanche of Castille.

In the Rue Lainerie, at number 14, is the Maison Mayet de Beauvoir, which is built in the Flamboyant Gothic style, but whose carved medallions on the front are evidence of a Renaissance influence. Almost at the corner of the Place Saint-Paul, at the foot of a corbelled tower, a plaque recalls the fact that it was here, in the early 19th century, that Laurent Mourguet invented the puppet, Guignol, which still performs today in various places, including the Palais Bondy next door.

Turn left into the Rue Juiverie (Street of the Jews), whose name denotes that this is the banking district, the lending of money for interest being theoretically forbidden to Catholics. In 1993, the city council designated it the 'rue des artisans d'art' (street of craftsmen) because of the number of craftsmen who have decided to live there. Forty coats of arms belonging to medieval city dignitaries have been placed in the street as a reminder of the old shop signs. Very beautiful houses stand side by side here, including, at number 4, the Maison Henri IV, where a bust of the king has been rather belatedly placed in the courtyard, and the Hôtel Paterin, which is a very large Renaissance house that was

The Villa Florentine is a luxury hotel that has been built in the former convent of the Filles de la Providence (Daughters of Providence) at 25, montée Saint-Barthélemy.

altered in 1752, and which lost part of its buildings when a now-abandoned funicular station was built. At number 8, the Hôtel Bullioud (Bullioud was a 'général des finances' during the reign of François I) was made from four houses being knocked together. In 1535, its owner asked the architect, Philibert Delorme, who had just come back from Italy, to construct a gallery in his house, and this marvel of grace and balance, inspired by the decoration of the theatre of Marcellus in Rome, can be seen after passing through a first courtyard and then an arched passageway. In the design of the two turrets built on squinches, Delorme has used Doric deco-

Guignol

Laurent Mouguet started life as a silk worker, but, following the Revolution, he did many different jobs, including that of a tooth puller in Lyons' public squares. In order to distract his patients at the crucial moment, he played with traditional puppets, but found in the end that glove puppets were the more entertaining, and so decided to stick with them. He created a puppet that looked like him and to which he gave the name, Guignol, the origin of which is the subject of much controversy, and then he created another puppet which looked like his friend, Thomas Ladré, who loved to drink, and which was christened Gnafron. A third puppet was a woman, Madelon, and was based on his own wife. He played in the cafés and at the fairs in the region, and his dialogues, which, apart from the basic framework, were often improvised, were based on everyday life in the city. The golden age of Guignol theatre was in the late 19th century, but the tradition has continued up to the present day.

ration on the first floor, followed by Ionic decoration on the second, just as he later did at the Château d'Anet. At number 23, opposite the Ruelle Punaise, which is a real open-air sewer, the large house with lions is a lovely example of a 17th century building, with its front decorated with Florentine bosses, its flat mullions, the double-access well, and the half-spiral, half-straight-landing staircase. The origin of the animals that are scattered around the front of the house cannot be confirmed.

At the end of the Rue Juiverie, with the Montée du Change on the right, turn left and then right into the Rue du Boeuf, whose name comes from the statue of a bull by Hendric standing at number 13. This street also contains many very fine buildings, of which the largest is the Hôtel de Gadagne, the result of the joining together, by the extremely rich Florentine Gadagne family, of two buildings constructed by Nicolas and André de Pierrevive. It now houses Lyons' 'Musée Historique' (Historical Museum) and

Part of the interior courtyard of the Cour des Loges luxury hotel, that has been built in the outbuildings of the former Collège Notre-Dame at 6, rue du Boeuf.

The Hôtel Bullioud's very handsome gallery is the work of Philibert Delorme.

23

Musée de la Marionette' (Puppet Museum). After laying dormant for a long time, restoration and reconstruction work is in full flow. Archaeological excavations have been carried out, the gardens and small courtyard are open to the public, and the collections, of which many items today are in store, displayed.

The Montée du Garillan leads to the Montée Saint-Barthélemy, where, at number 25, there is a luxurious villa, the Villa Florentine, which used to be the 'Couvent des Pauvres Filles de Providence' (Convent of the Poor Girls of Providence), of which the side facing the Saône is superb, and from whose gardens a magnificent view of the city can be enjoyed. Go back down to the 5th 'arrondissement' (administrative subdivision)'s town hall, which occupies the former Collège Notre-Dame given by Gabrielle de Gardagne to the Jesuits in 1630. Go inside to admire the handsome spiral staircase that rests upon four newels. The restored outbuildings are now the Cour des Loges luxury hotel (at number 6), where three parts of the building, of which two have galleries overlooked by the bedrooms, frame a glass-roofed courtyard which is used as the reception area. Just opposite, a courtyard with a straight staircase and railings on each floor that are made of attractive gilded wood is worth seeing. Number 14 was used as a real tennis court during the 15th and 16th centuries, thereby explaining the height of the ground floor next to the courtyard. At number 16, an extremely beautiful doorway is decorated with 17th century bosses, and is topped by a pediment depicting a religious scene. Through this can be entered a courtyard that is overlooked by hanging gardens, and in which stands a very prominent staircase tower. This Maison de la Tour Rose (House of the Pink Tower) or du Crible (Riddle or Sieve) was the first home of Philippe Chavent's restaurant, which has now moved into a former 15th century real tennis court at number 22. At number 19, the Maison de l'Outarde d'Or (Golden Bustard) has taken the name of an old inn that stood here in 1708. Here can be found all the architectural elements that are characteristic of the houses in this area, such as entrance by an arched passageway, galleries, staircase towers, small rooms on squinches or corbels, and the absence of any uniformity of style. At number 31, this 17th century house is the only one to have been able to stable horses and keep carriages, as it stands on a large plot of land at the junction of two streets, and has a carriage house and stables. Overlooking the courtyard, a U-shaped gallery-balcony serves the flats on the first floor, whereas there are only two sides on the second floor, and only one side on the third.

The Maison de l'Outarde d'Or (House of the Golden Bustard).

The houses of Old Lyons

Most are built on very narrow, long plots, like piano keys,
but they are, on the other hand, rather tall at three or four storeys high,
or even more, although some were certainly heightened later.
In general, they are built of cob, with stone only being used
for the foundations, the ground floor, and for framing the window, door,
and gateway openings. There are not many windows as the house fronts
are not very wide, but they occupy as large a space as possible
in order to let in the maximum amount of light to the rooms that opened
out onto the dark, narrow streets. (The roofs of the houses jut out a lot
over the walls of the houses in order to allow rainwater to pour down
into the channels in the middle of the streets). The importance
of each floor diminished the higher up it was, so the first floor
was where the owners of the property and their children lived, then,
at a greater or smaller distance away, lived the parents, and then,
under the roof, the servants. Apart from the windows and stone,
wooden, or wrought iron fanlights above the entrance doors,
the house fronts are plain, with very little in the way
of decorative detail.
Up to the 17th century, all the house plans were very much alike,
even if modifications in design were sometimes necessary. The house
was entered by a passageway that was generally arched and situated
either to the left or right of the main front. At the end of this passage
was a courtyard, whose size varied from house to house, as well as
two blocks of buildings, one where the main front faced the street
that had just been left, and the other which only looked onto
the courtyard. However, sometimes, the second building had its
own main front that overlooked a parallel street. In this case,
a second passageway led to the courtyard, and access could be
gained from one street to another by using this 'traboule'.
In the courtyard, there was usually a well where, early
in the morning, the servants came to fetch the water that was
so necessary in the life of the household. A tower, of varying design,
was built in a corner of the courtyard or sometimes in the middle
of the wall that connected the two parts of the building, and this housed
a spiral staircase, with, at the top, a space that might have been used
for keeping a lookout for enemies, or for having a breath of fresh air,
or for hanging out the washing to dry, or for declaring the owner's social
standing. As the flight of stairs served both parts of the building,
a gallery on each floor gave access to the rooms facing the tower. During
the 17th century, the house fronts became wider and the windows more

numerous, with four to six for each floor, arranged on either side
of a tower enclosing straight staircases from which landings served
each floor. They were also built in a wider range of styles,
and were decorated with mouldings
or pediments. The courtyard ceased to exist,
as did the second part of the house that was built
onto the courtyard.

SAINT-PAUL

The construction of the railway station, the Quais de Bondy and Pierre Scize, the Rue Octavio Mey, and the Place Saint-Paul, all of which was planned to ease the flow of traffic and to link the station with the Pont du Change and Pont de la Feuillée, cut this district off from the others in Old Lyons and led to the demolition of a lot of houses. The recently restored station dates from 1873, and serves the west of the Lyons area with mainly regional services.

At the heart of the area is the ancient church of Saint-Paul, which used to belong to the 24 canons of the extremely rich and powerful Chapter of Saint-Paul. A church has stood on this site since Merovingian times, and around it grew up a semi-rural town, enclosed by its own walls, and living independently from the rest of the city. This continued until the 13th century when a large influx of population was attracted to Saint-Paul by the stone bridge, the port, and the bank. Merchants established themselves in the area in the 14th and 15th centuries, and stayed there all during the Renaissance. The church of Saint-Laurent was built next to the church of Saint-Paul, and it was here that

The Maisons Mangini,
which run from
85 to 90, quai Pierre Scize,
are the forerunners of
present-day council housing

Saint-Paul's station dates from 1873.

the theologian, Jean Gerson, was buried in 1429.

The church of Saint-Paul has undergone many alterations. Archbishop Leidrade restored it in about 800, it was rebuilt in the 11th century, and then remodelled and enlarged between the late 12th and late 13th centuries. Important alterations also took place in the 15th century. From 1778 to 1781, the church buildings were completely reconstructed but kept to the former plan, for example, there is still part of the 12th century structure in the north transept and in the last bay of the nave. Further restoration work was carried out in the 19th century. The present church therefore has a Romanesque plan, but the various alterations that it has undergone has made architectural interpretation difficult. Outside, the octagonal dome decorated with two rows of arcading separated by small columns dates from the 12th century, and also Romanesque in date are the medallions depicting monsters, animals, heads of bearded men, and women that support the upper cornice of the nave and the side door's archivolt. The church steeple was erected in the 15th century, and the 19th century saw the addition of the skylight at the top of the dome as well as the porch, whose tympanum depicts St Paul on the road to Damascus. Inside, the east of the nave has semi-circular Romanesque arches, whilst those of the west are arches made of intersecting ribs. The choir and oven-vaulted apse are 14th century. The most striking part is the dome built on squinches, where two octagons fit together and rise up to the keystone from which hangs a dove. The chapels are also a mixture of styles, with those on the right that are dedicated to St Francis Xavier and St Joseph, as well as the fonts, being Gothic. 17th and 18th century paintings decorate several chapels and the arms of the transept, while a 19th century fresco in the choir is attributed to the Lyons spiritualist school. The 20th century stained glass windows in the arms of the transept depict the martyrs of Lyons. The church of Saint-Laurent was demolished in 1793.

Several other beautiful old houses are to be found in the Rue Saint-Paul, the Rue Dugros, and the Quai Pierre Scize. At the end of the Rue Saint-Paul, the houses at numbers 85, 86, 87, 88, 89, and 90 on the quayside were built in the late 19th century by the 'Service des Logements Economiques et d'Alimentation' (Economic Accommodation and Food Service), presided over by Félix Mangini, and were the forerunners of present-day council housing.

One of Old Lyons' sunny pavement cafés in the Place Saint-Paul.

SAINT-GEORGES

The district of Saint-Georges is more modest and less well-kept than those of Saint-Jean and Saint-Paul, and for a long time has been the poor relation of this Renaissance area. Lying between the Montée de Choulans, where the Fourvière tunnel begins, and the Rue du Doyenné, it is a genuinely working-class area where generation after generation of craftsmen and workers lived up to the mid-19th century. Its obvious attractiveness is wholly due to its houses that cling onto the hillside, its very attractive 'montées', such as the vertiginous Montée des Epies, that joins up with the Montée du Gourgillon, which dates from the Roman period and so is one of the oldest streets in Lyons, and its lovely shady riverside.

Starting from the Place Saint-Jean, both the Rue Tramassac and Rue du Doyenné lead into the district of Saint-Georges.

The ancient church of Saint-Paul was altered many times until the 19th century.

The southern part of Old Lyons, where the Saint-Georges area runs alongside the river Saône.

PLACE DE LA TRINITÉ

The Fathers of the Order of the Trinity established themselves here in 1664, but the fact that this attractive small square is well-known to so many of the people of Lyons is due to the fact that Laurent Mourget, the father of Guignol, loved to use it as part of his scenery. He also featured prominently the Maison du Soleil (House of the Sun – now the Café du Soleil), which was inhabited in the 18th century by the family of the Baron du

The picturesque Montée de Gourgillon which climbs up the hillside to Fourvière.

Soleil, who had his sign carved over the door. There are two niches high up on the house, one on each corner, that hold a statue of the Virgin Mary (left-hand corner) and St Peter (right-hand corner). After walking round the café by the Rue Saint-Georges, the Maison du Soleil's handsome front door, decorated with a fanlight of turned wood, can be admired at number 2. If, by chance, the front door and gate are open (which is highly unlikely), it will be seen that there is an extremely original stairwell, which is a magnificent oval pool of light encircled by metal banisters.

Before continuing along the Rue Saint-Georges, several metres of the Montée du Gouguillon, to the height of numbers 5 to 7, must be climbed so as to see the area's oldest house, standing at the foot of the Impasse Turquet. The house was built during the Middle Ages, and still has its exterior wooden gallery, evidence of its miraculous survival in spite of a series of fires.

RUE SAINT-GEORGES

The area's main thoroughfare displays several architectural details that are characteristic of the Renaissance, for example, a carved capercaillie near number 5, paired windows and trefoil arches at number 7, menacing lions baring their fangs on the front of number 11, a spiral staircase at number 29 (behind the glass door), and mullioned windows at number 31. A few craftsmen, who are few and far between in the street, carry on the memory of the former potters, tilers, Saône boatmen, tanners, and weavers that used to live and work in Saint-Georges.

CHURCH OF SAINT-GEORGES

This small building was constructed in 1844 by Pierre Bossan on the ruins of a previous church, the old church of the Convent of Sainte-Eulalie, that had been completely destroyed by fire and whose origins went back to the 6th century. More than thirty years before his most famous work, the church at Fourvière, the Lyons architect adopted the neo-Gothic style here, not only in the architecture but also in the furnishings which he designed himself.

Go round the church to go down towards the Quai Fulchiron and the Place Benoît Crépu. The eye is immediately drawn towards the beautiful, finely-carved

facade of the building at number 7 that stands at the corner of the quay. It is neo-Moorish in style, and is also the work of Bossan, who built it in 1846 very shortly after the church of Saint-Georges.

A row of Renaissance houses and their mullioned windows in the Rue Saint-Georges.

QUAI FULCHIRON

In the 16th century, the former Quai de la Commanderie was the location of the Commanderie (commander's residence) de Saint-Georges, which belonged to the Knights of Malta, and gave its name to the whole of the area. Today, it is a lovely place to take a walk, whether on the Old Lyons or the Saône side. Opposite the church, a 75 metre long footbridge crosses the river, and affords one of the best views of the area.

Remains of the late 5th century church of Saint-Laurent have been found at the end of the Quai Fulchiron at number 41, and some pieces of its architecture can be seen under the 'Highway' block of flats at the corner of the quay and the Montée de Choulans. Projecting out over the quay, the Rue de la Quarantaine has been called so since the 15th century, during which a hospital for plague victims, i.e. those who had to remain in 'quarantine', was constructed, and which remained in use until the mid-16th century.

The Saint-Georges footbridge, a beautiful link between the Saint-Georges area and the Peninsula.

The former 'Quai de la Commanderie' is now the Quai Fulchiron.

29

The banks of the Saône

CHAPTER 3

Across from one bank to another, the Saône gives Lyons its most beautiful viewpoints and a large part of its attractive charm. The coloured house fronts with their lines of windows, the bridges and footbridges suspended over the river as if by magic, and the meanders of the Saône that reveal superb views of the city with, as a backdrop, the hills of Croix-Rousse or Fourvière, are real incentives to go for a lovely walk from the Pont de la Feuillée in Saint-Paul up to the Pont Général Koenig just before Vaise.

HOMME DE LA ROCHE
(MAN OF THE ROCK)

The Quai Pierre Scize was laid out rather belatedly in the 19th century, and has preserved few traces of the 16th and 17th centuries, but the very fine block of flats at number 110, which was formerly an 18th century house, is worth a look. The quay also carefully preserves the only bridge over the Saône which was not destroyed by bombs during the Second World War. Today it is a footbridge that goes by the name of the 'Homme de la Roche', who was François

Opposite:
The peaceful charm of the banks of the Saône.

Barges on the Saône: a real little port in the very centre of Lyons.

Markets and 'bouquinistes' (second-hand booksellers)

'Bouquinistes' set up their stalls on the Quai de la Pécherie on the left bank of the Saône every afternoon, thus turning the area into one large open-air bookshop, specialising in antiquarian books and old postcards. On Sunday mornings, the Marché de la Création on the Quai Romain Rolland and the Marché de l'Artisanat (Craft Market) on the Quai Fulchiron, stretch out on the opposite bank, with a lot of painters, all sorts of sculptors and artists, jewellers, and craftsmen in wood, leather, cloth, and pottery.

The classical architecture of the Conservatoire National Supérieur de Musique (National Music Conservatoire) stands just above waters of the river Saône.

I's chief valet of the bedchamber, and then a banker and benefactor of the poor in Lyons. His statue, which nestles in a grotto in the tiny Place de l'Homme de la Roche that faces the bridge, was carved in 1849 by Bonnaire, who, it is said, took his inspiration from a portrait by Dürer.

CONSERVATOIRE NATIONAL SUPÉRIEUR DE MUSIQUE (MUSIC CONSERVATOIRE)

A few dozen metres further along the Quai Cheveau lies the beautiful classical architecture of the former convent of the Sisters of Sainte-Elisabeth, which was the subject of alterations in the 19th century, and which now houses Lyons'

Festival of Lights

At dusk on the 8th December each year, the people of Lyons place small candles on their window sills, thereby giving the city its most beautiful Christmas decoration. This festival was at first religious in that it is a tribute paid to the Virgin Mary since 1852, but it has broadened its scope over the years, and has quite recently been transformed into a real festival of lights. Over several days, the city council, with the help of several private sponsors, illuminates the 'traboules', the quays by the side of the Saône and the Rhône, and historical, religious, and public buildings. Everybody gets together in the streets in the evening to admire this special kind of firework which so beautifully lights up Lyons.

Conservatoire National Supérieur de Musique. It was also the home of the first veterinary school in France, founded by Claude Bourgelat in 1763.

Cross the Saône by the Pont de Général Koenig, glancing over to the imposing Fort Saint-Jean that was built in 1830 on Croix-Rousse hill.

GRENIER D'ABONDANCE (GRANARY OF PLENTY)

Immediately to the right at the very beginning of the Quai Saint-Vincent, the handsome rectangular building is the former 'grenier d'abondance', built in 1722 as a grain store. At that time, grain supplies were transported to the city by boat, and it was therefore decided to construct municipal granaries right next to the Saône in order to make the unloading of the sacks of wheat easier and its theft impossible. Today, the Direction Régionale des Affaires Culturelles (Regional Cultural Affairs Service) is housed in the restored building, which can be visited during the Journées de la Patrimone (Historical and Cultural Heritage Days – two days in September each year when France throws open the doors, free of charge, of a large number and a great variety of its historic buildings, of which many, as here, can only be visited by the public at this time).

LES SUBSISTANCES

A little further along the quay, the large group of ochre-coloured buildings with their attractive arcading has taken on a whole new life thanks to a comprehensive restoration project which took three years to complete. This old 17th century convent was converted into a barracks in the 19th century, and was used as a food storehouse (hence the name) during the First World War. It was purchased by the City of Lyons in 1995, and today welcomes a wide variety of artists in its new role as an arts centre.

The Saône was a very busy navigable waterway in the 18th century.

A sunbathing session on the Quai de la Pêcherie.

The very ornate pediment of the former Grenier d'Abondance bears witness to the building's previous use.

The Presqu'île (Peninsula)

CHAPTER 4

The Presqu'île has, above anything else, always been 'the town' to the people of Lyons, and even after the construction of La Part-Dieu, which was meant to create a new city centre, going 'to town' always means going to that part of Lyons between the Saône and the Rhône. In an area of about 5 kilometres long and between 600 to 800 metres wide from the Place des Terreaux to Perrache is situated such a large concentration of shops, department stores, bookshops, theatres, cinemas, art galleries, cafés, and restaurants that there is something to appeal to everybody. The fact that this should be the case is remarkable because the physical nature of the site was hardly favourable for human occupation, as there used to be water everywhere, with the confluence of the Rhône and Saône being at the level of the present church of Ainay, and islands clogging up the rivers which were continually changing their course, leaving behind areas of marshland on the areas over which they had flowed. However, merchants did settle in the southern part, called Canabae, during the Roman period, as is shown by about sixty mosaics and numerous other objects unearthed here. During the Middle Ages, apart from the northern churches of Saint-Nizier, Saint-Pierre, Saint-Saturnin, and Notre-Dame-de-la-Platière, the population gradually moved southwards down to the Pont de la Guillotière, with development around the southern nucleus of the abbey of Saint-Martin-d'Ainay and the oratory of Saint-Michel not making much progress because of the large amount of property owned by the abbey. It was therefore not until early modern times, when the abbots divided their gardens up for sale, that the city extended down to the south, and even increased in size thanks to the engineer,

Perrache, who drained the land to push back the confluence of the two rivers to La Mulatière and join the islands together to form solid ground. It was left to more recent times to remodel the whole area in order to ease the flow of traffic by carving major thoroughfares through the medieval part, in the style of Hausmann in Paris, building the Perrache railway station, and constructing the motorway, the underground, and the tramway, as well as pedestrianised areas, to show off to its best advantage an architectural and historical heritage that has been amassed over two thousand years and recognised by 20 listings and 58 registrations in the Inventaire Supplémentaire des Monuments Historiques (Supplementary List of Historic Buildings).

Needless to say, this 'city centre' has had an eventful history which has witnessed the disappearance of many buildings. It is quite common to find buildings, including houses,

Opposite:
The largest square in Europe, the Place Bellecour, stands in the middle of the Presqu'île.

Flower stalls stand underneath the chestnut trees on the south side of the Place Bellecour.

because the Presqu'île is also a residential area, of different periods standing next door to each other. Two parts have quite clearly acquired their own particular characteristics, and, as they both hinge on the Place Bellecour, it is a good idea to start there.

PLACE BELLECOUR

At 500 metres long and between 220 and 280 metres wide, this square really does form 'the centre of the centre'. It is the most important meeting-place in

Standing imposingly on its pedestal in the centre of the square is the statue of Louis XIV by Lemot.

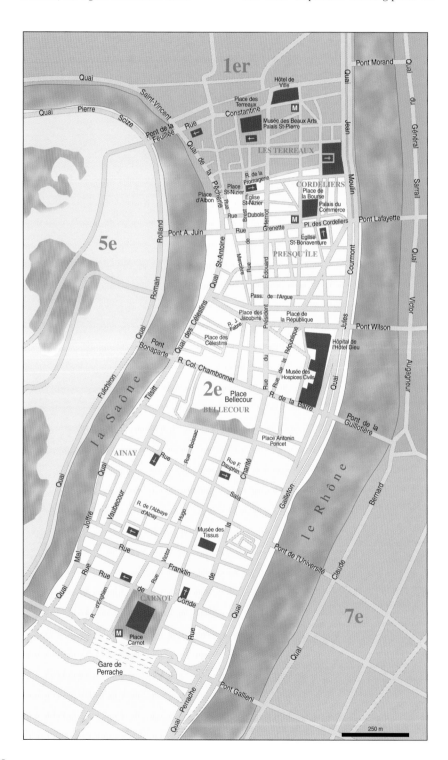

Lyons, and the arrival and departure point for most demonstrations. It is also the point from which all distances are calculated. This former area of marshland was used as a rubbish dump in the Middle Ages, but became an enclosed area bearing the name of Belle Cour after its purchase by the archbishop. The Protestants set up camp here in 1562, using it as a firing range for the arquebusiers, as noted by Henry IV, who recommended its purchase and had lime-trees planted along the south side. Louis XIII designated it a royal square, but nothing much was done about its layout until the reign of Louis XIV, whose statue used to stand imposingly in the centre. This statue was commissioned from Desjardins in 1688, cast in 1694, loaded onto a boat at Le Havre in 1700, reached its destination in Lyons via Gibraltar, Toulon, and the Rhône Valley in 1701, was placed on a pedestal decorated with statues of the Rhône and Saône based on models by the Coustou brothers, and was finally inaugurated in 1715. At the eastern and western ends of the square were built five houses which actually form only one frontage, and which were designed by Robert de Cotte, whereas the houses to the north and south do not have the same uniformity of character. A fountain and some pools erected around the statue and put into

A procession during the biennial dance festival.

The Place Bellecour is at the very heart of the 20th century city.

The private mansions of the 17th and 18th centuries are concentrated between Bellecour and Perrache.

Statues representing the Rhône and Saône decorate the pedestal of Louis XIV's statue.

operation, with water from the Rhône, by the hydraulic engineer, Petitot, under Delamonce's supervision, helped to make the square the very pleasantest of places for a walk and the home of the city's social elite. However, Louis XIV's statue was demolished and melted down in 1792, and Coustou's statues were moved to the town hall. The facades to the east and west of the square were destroyed as a punishment to the city that dared to rebel against the ruling power in Paris, and the Place Louis-le-Grand became the Place Egalité, where opponents of the Revolution were shot. During the time of the Consulate, Napoleon Bonaparte laid the first stone of the identical reconstruction of the destroyed house fronts, and during the Restoration period, Lemot sculpted another equestrian statue, which was rejoined in 1953 by the statues of the Rhône and Saône. Chestnut trees have now replaced the lime-trees, and an open-air café, flower stalls, and two buildings (the eastern one being the tourist office), have sprung up in the south of the square. In addition, ever since 1945, the monument of the 'Veilleur de Pierre' (Stone Lookout) by Salendre at the corner of the Rue Gasparin has paid tribute to five people from

Lyons who were shot on this site during the German Occupation. Nevertheless, it can be said that the Place Bellecour has now regained the appearance that it had during the Ancien Régime.

The Place Antonin Poncet links the Place Bellecour to the Rhône. A bell-tower, which might have been rebuilt according to a plan by Bernini, is all that remains of the large hospital of La Charité that was built in the early 17th century for the shutting away of the poor, and demolished in 1934 by the city council led by the then mayor, Edouard Herriot. Tree-lined lawns are separated from the traffic by some railings that lead to an illuminated fountain with jets of variable heights of water as well as to an, as yet, little used landing stage. The Post Office, which occupies part of the old Charité site to the south, was built of reinforced concrete in a very plain and simple style between 1935 and 1938 by Roux-Spitz. Twenty-four bas-reliefs depicting Lyons' history decorate the entrance doors, while the interior of the room open to the public is dominated by a 54 metre-long mosaic by Louis Bouquet, featuring the city's influence and technical progress, as well as far-flung countries. To the north, between the Quai Gailleton and the Rue des Marroniers, the luxury Rigaud de Terrebasse flats were built by François Desarnod in about 1772. The Rue des Marroniers is a pedestrian street, where there are lots of restaurants and 'bouchons' (small, simple, traditional Lyons restaurants).

There are two itineraries through the area, both of which start from the Place Bellecour.

FROM BELLECOUR TO PERRACHE

The southern route takes in the medieval Ainay Abbey, Lyons' town planning and the 17th and 18th century hôtels (town houses), two important museums, the changes brought about during the 20th century, and the very special atmosphere prevailing in an area that used to be inhabited by the city's elite. As the area was divided up for sale by the abbots of Ainay, whose names have been given to the streets that they marked out, the street network here is very regular, and it is therefore very easy to find your way around.

The first private mansions stand around the edge of the Place Bellecour. At number 8, rue Bloissac, the 17th century Hôtel de Fleurieu-Claret de la Tourette, which today is the Ecole du Sacré-Coeur, has kept its courtyard and garden structure, while inside, the staircase has a ceiling painted by Daniel Sarrabat in 1695, entitled 'Psyche gazing upon sleeping Love'. At number 2, rue Auguste Lecomte, the Hôtel de Varey, whose ground floor rooms are open to the public for cultural events as it houses the Espace Bellecour, was built in 1758 by Loyer.

In the same street, at number 11, the church of Saint-François-de-Sales was constructed between 1807 and 1847 by Claude-Anthelme Benoît in a neo-Gothic style, and decorated later with frescoes by Janmot under the dome and with statues by Fabisch. The doorway of the baptistery at 12, rue François Dauphin is ornamented by a 1640 pediment salvaged from the former convent of the Visitation-Notre-Dame-des-Chaînes on the Quai des Sereins. At numbers 9 and 11 of the same street, the Hôtel de l'Intendance of 1670 has a beautiful double flight of stairs and a shady, cobbled courtyard.

The Rue François Dauphin ends in the Rue de la Charité, where, at numbers 12 and 14, stands the 'Nouvelliste' building, erected in 1893 by Malaval and decorated by Millefaut to house the offices of the conservative Catholic newspaper founded by Joseph Rambaud. It has a large statue of Joan of Arc together with a lion waving a banner which bears the motto 'Dieu et Patrie' (God and Country).

The Rue François Dauphin runs alongside the church of Saint-François-de-Sales and the Hôtel de l'Intendance.

The siege of Lyons

On 29 May, 1793, a revolt drove out the left-wing extremist Montagnards, who also enjoyed the support of the people of Paris, from Lyons City Council, which then became more moderate and Girondin in sympathy. In Paris, on the 31 May and 2 June, 1793, 29 Girondin members were arrested at the Convention, which from then on was under Montagnard control. This difference of opinion was fatal to Lyons, which appeared to be a centre of opposition in a country at war and a prey to federalist movements, right at the time of the royalist Chouan uprising in the Vendée. The Convention army laid siege to Lyons from 8 August, and the city was forced to surrender on 9 October, consequently suffering extremely harsh repressive action organised by Fouché and Collot d'Herbois. A decree of 12 October changed Lyons' name to that of 'Ville Affranchie' (liberated city), opponents' houses were demolished, and after summary trials, the condemned were shot on the Plaine des Brotteaux. This memory still haunts the old Lyons families, some of whom never go to the Place des Terreaux where the revolutionary tribunal was set up in the Hôtel de Ville, and it is one of the factors in the hostility felt by the people of Lyons towards the people of Paris.

The Rue de la Charité cuts across the Rue Sala, where at numbers 42 and 44 is a beautiful 'traboule' called the 'Cours des Fainéants' (Idlers' Court), which has a double passageway decorated with pink and green stucco and in whose cobbled courtyard is a stone single-storey building which houses some craftsmen's workshops. The 'traboule' comes out at numbers 29 and 31, rue Sainte-Hélène, and just opposite, at number 30, is the Hôtel de Cuzieu, built in about 1759, which stands between its courtyard and garden. The garden frontage is more elaborate than that of the courtyard. A magnificent Louis XV staircase leads to the lovely suites of rooms in which Madame Yemeniz, the daughter of an important printing family and the wife of a silk manufacturer / merchant of Greek origin, held a salon supporting the pretender to the French throne, and which was the cradle of liberal Catholicism. The modern glass-fronted building at the side houses the Maison de l'Environnement, which groups together several environmental organisations.

Turn right back onto the Rue de la Charité. At number 17, the 1753 Hôtel de Nervo is built on a triangular piece of land on which a terrace used as a garden has been built, while its carriage entrance is very elegantly decorated. At number 30, the 1739 Hôtel Lacroix-Laval is attributed to Soufflot, and on its three floors, the magnificent collections of the Musée des Arts Décoratifs (Museum of Decorative Arts) have been displayed, in the perfect setting, since 1925. At number 34 is the Hôtel des Villeroy, built by

The Musée des Tissus relates the history of textiles worldwide, from the 4th century to the present-day.

Bertaud de la Vaure in 1730, and home of the governors of Lyons up to the Revolution. The 'Musée de Tissus' (Textile Museum) was founded in 1856 in order to give a fresh boost to the Lyons silk industry, and was transferred here in 1946 by the Chamber of Commerce. Here, textiles from all over the world, dating from the 4th century to the present-day, are displayed, although, of course, the Lyons silk industry is given pride of place. The most important of France's textile museums also has a library, a restoration workshop for antique fabrics, and the Centre International d'Etudes des Textiles Anciens

(International Centre for Antique Fabrics).

Take the cobbled Rue de Fleurieu, which runs at an angle alongside the Hôtel de Nervo and leads to the Place Gailleton, and which was laid out in the 18th century at the time of the first construction works in Perrache. A monument was erected here in 1913 in memory of the former mayor and the work that he had carried out. A lot of res-

The Hôtel des Villeroy (1730) has housed the Musée des Tissus since 1946. The museum was created in 1856 by the city's Chamber of Commerce.

The Place Carnot today.

taurants and art galleries are clustered around the square, where a lovely late 18th century house stands at the corner of the Quai Gailleton.

Further along the quay is the junction with the Rue des Remparts d'Ainay, a reminder that the abbey used to have its own walls, and which is home numerous craftsmen have set up their workshops there. Take the Rue de la Charité on the left to see, at number 46, the main part of the Hôtel de Sarron, which is decorated with two bas-reliefs and was designed by Jean Maigre. It is hidden behind a 19th century building with a very attractive main front.

Take the Rue Franklin to the right where, at number 57, is an 1840 building with two wings, a monumental doorway, and an iron gate closing off a courtyard lined with stables, and, at number 10, a neo-Renaissance house which was the home of the architect and writer, Clair Tisseur, who, under the name of Nizier du Puits Pelu, wrote the 'Littré de la Grande Côte' on the subject of the Lyonnais dialect. He designed the town house opposite for an industrial company, and this, after some alterations by Hirsch between 1890 and 1893, became the 2nd 'arrondisement''s town hall. The church of Sainte-

Croix, built in 1873 by Boirou, stands in the next street, the Rue de Condé, which leads into the Place Carnot.

There is a certain nostalgia among the older people of Lyons for the beautiful old square with its monument to the Republic in the middle, and which ended in the south with the large expanse of the Cours de Verdun and its two curving monumental staircases leading up to Perrache railway station, all of which disappeared in 1976. Today, access ramps of pink sandstone and stepped ornamental pools have appeared in the middle of the square, leading up to the Centre d'Echanges (Trade Centre) that was built between 1972 and 1976 by Gagé, Prouvé, and Vanderaa to serve as both a coach and metro station, and also as an interchange for the Autoroute du Soleil (Motorway to the Sun), which links Paris to the south of France. A shopping centre, offices, exhibition halls, which include the Espace Lyonnais d'Art Contemporain (Lyons Gallery of Contemporary Art), conference rooms and a superb roof-garden have also been added. Entrance to Perrache station, which was built in 1857 and altered in 1982, is by footbridge. Peynot's group of statues representing the 'ville educatrice' (city of education) has been taken away

41

The houses of the Presqu'île

Several medieval or 16th century houses, similar to those in Old Lyons, can still be found on the Presqu'île, e.g. in the Rue Mercière. During the 17th and 18th centuries, there were three different types of houses. The private 'hôtel', or mansion (to be found mainly between Bellecour and Perrache) was the preserve of the city's wealthy elite. Imitating Parisian models, only with less space and less money, they first appeared in the 17th century and continued to be built until the end of the Ancien Régime. The most luxurious of them stood between a courtyard, separated from the street by a wall with a carriage entrance, and a garden, their decoration following the changing fashions of the period. The luxury apartment building enabled the less wealthy elite to live aloof from the masses in extremely comfortable accommodation. The block was entered by a large carriage entrance, which then lead to a passage on which stood a staircase, and which opened out onto a large courtyard of varying shape, which was overlooked by some of the flats and where horses and carriages could be left. There were no shops on the ground floor, and the usual arrangement was that of one high-ceilinged and richly-panelled flat per floor. This is the case with the apartment buildings in Bellecour, the Rue du Plat, the Rue Royale, and the Quais Lassagne and Jules Courmont. Others lived in varying sizes of rented flats, where the owner might also live,

where the flats were not necessarily on the same level, and where the tenants had to comply with the demands of the chief tenant, who looked after the flats' finances for the owner, and after its good behaviour in respect of the authorities. In the 19th century, most of the apartment buildings were built for renting. Their fronts are decorated according to period taste, as recommended by the Société d'Architecture de Lyon, with designs displayed in collections, and brought into general use by industrially produced decorative designs in cast iron. The taste for the neo-Classical style, with its triangular or curved pediments, pilasters, columns, friezes of Grecian frets, palmettes, coronas, arrows, and lyres, lasted until the 1840s, when pointed arches, sirens, centaurs, troubadours, medallions of faces, and griffins made their appearance. During the Second Empire, the decoration spread to the whole façade, often being prepared in advance for balconies, window and door frames, and street corners, while the number of different figures increased still further, with putti (cherubs), male and female caryatids, figures of Mercury carrying symbols of life in Lyons, lions' heads, and garlands of flowers and fruits. The more the century advanced, the heavier the decoration became, until the Art Deco style brought about a greater simplicity of style.

and dismantled, and the other statues that used to stand here are in a public garden at Montchat. However, some beautiful 19th century buildings line the square, numbers 5, 6, 12, 13, 16, and 20 being particularly worthy of attention, as well as the hotels and restaurants catering for the needs of travellers. The Brasserie Georges, at 30, cours de Verdun, was built in 1836, and has a 1930s décor with rural paintings by Guillermin and some bas-reliefs. The Château Perrache (the former terminus) at 12, cours de Verdun, was erected by Georges Chedanne in 1905, and is the biggest single Art Nouveau site in the city.

From the Place Carnot, the abbey of Saint-Martin-d'Ainay is reached by way of the Rue de Condé and the Rue d'Enghien. It is not certain whether it was built on the burial ground where the remains of Sainte Blandine and the other martyrs of 177 used to be worshipped, but it is known that it existed in the 9th century, prospered throughout the whole of the Middle Ages, acquired a palace for its abbot in the 14th century, and attracted people to live around it. It was surrounded by walls, which were destroyed in 1777, but of which a single gate, the 'Voûte d'Ainey (Ainey Arch) remains, overlooking the Saône. In 1562, the abbey was badly damaged by the Protestants, and, as a result, never really rose up from the ruins before the Revolution destroyed it almost completely, leaving only the church, which is the result of many different stages of construction. A Carolingian building was succeeded by a 12th century church, to which was added a porch in the 15th century, and the whole lot was altered in the 19th century, thus making its architectural interpretation rather difficult.

From the outside, the church is Romanesque, of medium size, and rather plain, with diamond-shaped red brickwork contrasting with the white stone. On top of the porch, whose archivolt contains some very old carvings, stands a tower with arcading, some of which is blind, and a frieze of animals under the cornice between the second and third floors. The roof is decorated with four pyramidal crowns, and the two side doors are 19th century in date. Above the transept crossing, a square tower is finished off with some paired arcading. Two rows of six pillars divide the church into three, receiving the ribbed stone arches of the central and side vaulting which replaced the timber construction in the 19th century. The next four pillars, in red marble, come from the Roman altar of the Three Gauls, and sup-

port a dome on squinches in the transept crossing. The transept is not very distinctive, but has two chapels, the neo-Gothic Flamboyant chapel of Saint-Michel to the north, and the Romanesque chapel of Sainte-Blandine, which is raised up because of the fact that it is built over the crypt. The short apse, with a chapel on each side, has carved friezes, including the 'Agneau Mystique' (Mystic Lamb) on its walls. Carved Romanesque capitals in the choir depict, to the north, Cain and Abel, St Michael striking down the dragon, the murder of Abel, and

The fresco in the apse of the church of Saint-Martin-d'Ainay depicts the central figure of Christ with St Blandine, St Catherine, St Michael, St Pothin, and St Martin.

Above the transept crossing is a square tower topped with paired arcading.

St John the Baptist, and, in the south, Original Sin, Adam and Eve being turned out of the Garden of Eden, Christ in Majesty, and the Annunciation. These capitals date from the 11th and 12th centuries, as does the mosaic on the wall of Sainte-Blandine's chapel. On the other hand, the frescoes of Christ surrounded by the Virgin Mary, and Saints Blandine, Catherine, Michael, Pothin, and Martin in the apse, of Saints Benedict and Badulph in the side chapels, and of the Glorification of the Virgin Mary on the dome, as well as the painted vaulting, stained glass windows, and flooring, are all 19th century in date.

Go out of the church, glance at the neo-Gothic façade of the old presbytery at number 18, rue de l'Abbaye-d'Ainay, then turn left into the Rue Bourgelat, where, at number 19, can be seen the gateway of the riding ring of Claude Bourgelat, who founded the world's first veterinary school in 1762 in the suburb of La Guillotière. A wall-plaque on the corner with the Rue Adelaïde Perrin commemorates this fact. Follow this latter street up to the Rue Jarente, where at number 6, the Centre Adelaïde Perrin was built by Perrin in 1853 to accommodate sick people that the hospital could not keep. The chapel was built by his nephew, Sainte-Marie Perrin in 1896, and was the scene of the marriage of the architect's daughter and Paul Claudel, the writer, in 1906.

There is a choice of three ways back to the Place Bellecour. The pedestrianised Rue Victor Hugo is a lively shopping street with some fine buildings, particularly at numbers 10 and 14, which date from about 1845, number 16, which is Art Deco in style and which was built in 1934, and number 35. The Rue Auguste Comte is lined with antique shops. The Rue Vaubecour, which, after the Place Antoine Vallon and its attractive 1859 fountain, leads into the Rue du Plat, is quieter in atmosphere, and is the site of the Catholic university. At numbers 8 and 10, two twin oval courtyards are thought to be the work of Décrenice. The large synagogue at 13, quai Tilsit was built in 1863 by Abraham Hirsch, and at number 8, rue Alphonse Fochier is the birthplace of the writer and aviator, Antoine de Saint-Exupéry.

FROM THE PLACE BELLECOUR TO THE PLACE DES TERREAUX

Lyons' oldest public buildings are to be found in this area, but, on the other hand, old houses are rare as the area's redevelopment destroyed more than half the built-up area between 1840 and 1849.

Leave the Place Bellecour by the Rue de la Barre, coming to the Pont de la Guillotière, which replaced the old 12th century bridge over the Rhône in 1954, and from which the best view of the Hôtel-Dieu de Notre-Dame-de-la-Pitié is to be had. Whether there is any truth or not in the tradition that it goes back to the 6th century, a story given official status by the presence of statues of King Childebert and Queen Ultragoth on the main façade, this hospital was certainly built at the same time as the old bridge, at the end of the city's then central axis from the Rue Mercier to the Rue Confort, and on the site of the present chapel.

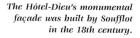

The Hôtel-Dieu's monumental façade was built by Soufflot in the 18th century.

This was where François Rabelais used to write, but nothing now remains of this building because the hospital's rectors, César Laure and Laurent Piquet, had it rebuilt between 1622 and 1636 in the shape of a cross, possibly inspired by the hospital in Milan, dominated by the Dôme des Quatre Rangs (Four Rows). The hospital chapel was built later between 1637 and 1653. However, by the early 18th century, the hospital was proving to be too small, and so the rectors bought some houses standing between the Hôtel-Dieu and the Rhône and then demolished them so that the hospital building could be extended alongside the river. Soufflot masterminded the subsequent construction, from 1739 to 1748, of an enormous, monumental building with its magnificent, though rather plain, 375 metre-long façade. A dome, whose principal functions were to let in fresh air and to enable it to circulate, was built between 1757 and 1764 by Toussaint Loyer, one of Soufflot's pupils, but had to be rebuilt in concrete during the 1960s as a result of damage suffered during the Second World War.

Take the Rue Bellecordière, which is a reminder of Louise Labbé, a 16th century Lyons poet, and the daughter and wife of rope-makers (cordiers), whose house stands at number 28, in order to see the Hôtel-Dieu's Louis XIII-style chapel with its 17th century statue of the Virgin and Child by Jacques Mimerel, which used to stand on the Pont du Change, the hospital's beautiful front door designed by Delamonce and decorated by Simon Guillaume in 1706, the cloister on the side of one arm of the cross, the interior of the new dome, and the Musée des Hospices Civils de Lyons (Museum of Lyons' Non-religious Hospices), which is housed in two of the four wards. Of special interest here are the three rooms that escaped the destruction of La Charité, the 18th century wood panelling in the Council Room, the beautiful oak cupboards in the archives room, the pharmacy cupboard, the 17th century apothecary's room, the painted pottery, tapestries, and medical instruments.

Take the Rue Rivière to the Place de la République, which has been stripped of the monument that was erected here in memory of President Carnot, who was assassinated not far from here in 1894, and which has now been replaced by a fountain. From here, the importance of the Rue Impériale's construction can be appreciated, as well as that of the Rue Président Carnot, which was laid out between 1890 and 1896 across the former island of Grolée. Further along the shop and department store-lined Rue de la République is the Place des Cordeliers, which takes its name from the Franciscan monastery which was established here in 1220, and of which only the church remains.

The church of Saint-Bonaventure is named after the Franciscans' minister general, who died during the 2nd Council of Lyon in 1274, and who is buried here. The present building dates from the 14th and 15th century, but was altered during the 17th, 18th, and 19th centuries. It is a heavy-looking, bulky building, an appearance that is accentuated by its flying buttresses. The main front is neo-Gothic and has a central porch bearing a carving of the Virgin and Child,

The painted ceiling in the Salle de la Corbeille of the Palais de Commerce depicts the city of Lyons, surrounded by the Virtues, presiding over the city's trading links with various nations.

Claude Marius Vaisse (1799–1864)

Vaisse came from Marseilles, and had a short but brilliant career under Louis-Philippe's July Monarchy, associated himself without any great enthusiasm to the Republic, but rapidly rejoined the prince-president's camp. He was a friend of the politician, Jean Persigny, who, on becoming Minister of the Interior in March, 1853, made him prefect of the Rhône and mayor of Lyons in March of the same year. He further achieved the position of senator in the December, 1853. His personality was hidden behind his work, as his aim was, above all, to get rid of politics from the city so that its management and business could flourish. Concepts of well-being, beautification, and practicality, as well as, strategic reasons, after the 1832 and 1834 silk-workers' revolts, governed the restoration of Lyons' city centre. It was easier to manoeuvre troops in the wide Rue Impériale, the Rue de l'Impératrice, and the Cours de Verdun, to assemble them in the large Place des Cordeliers and Place des Jacobins, and to move them into direct action thanks to the streets lying at right angles, such as the Rue de la Barre and Rue des Archers, than had been the case in the old, narrow medieval streets.

The buildings of the city's great banks stand one after another in the Rue de la République.

The Opéra (opera house) was built by Paul Chevenard in 1831 and given a new look by Jean Nouvel in 1993.

with St Bonaventure on one side and St Anthony of Padua on the other. The church's interior has a central nave, two side aisles, and some chapels, and has pointed Gothic arches over eight bays. The chapels are more elaborate, and some have Flamboyant Gothic arches. The stained glass windows are 19th and 20th century in date, and the 17th and 18th century paintings and Aubusson tapestries depict the story of St Bonaventure. It was here that the 1834 silk-workers' revolt came to an end, with the rebels being pursued right up to the altar, where they were slaughtered.

Opposite the church is the Palais du Commerce, built by Dardel between 1856 and 1862, which is Lyons' stock exchange and stockbrokers' headquarters, chamber of commerce, and commercial court. This building, whose style is best described as eclectic, draws from both Classical and Renaissance architecture with its interplay of slates and stones, while its metal ceilings and heating by means of stoves also made it very modern. Its central focus is the Stock Exchange, with its four corner buildings, and its staircases leading up to the northern and southern entrances. To the north, four male carya-

tids support the cornice of the pediment, where cupids display the city's coat of arms, whilst two women and two cherubs act as symbols of trade, shipping, industry, and applied art, while to the south, the imperial eagle stands under the clock, and two women carry symbols of plenty. A 1904 bas-relief by Vermare on the wall of the southern staircase depicts the Rhône and Saône. Inside, the central hall is encircled with galleries, and decorated with the coats of arms of the great financial centres, a frieze of sea monsters, 24 caryatids, and a painted ceiling where Lyons, surrounded by the virtues, presides over international trade. The Place de la Bourse has been laid out by the landscape architect, Chemetov.

In the Rue de la Bourse is the Lycée Ampère, the former Collège de la Trinité that was founded in 1519 and given to the Jesuits in 1565. Among the buildings designed by Father Martellange is the chapel of 1617, which was exquisitely decorated in the 18th century with a covering of different-coloured marble by Michel Perrache to a design by Delamonce, and which is where the formation of the Cisalpine Republic, the state formed in northern Italy by Napoleon, was proclaimed.

In the Rue de la République is a whole series of banks, including the Lyonnaise de Banque, built in 1865, at number 8, Crédit Lyonnaise, built in 1863, at number 18, and the Bank of France. The Rue de la République leads to the Opéra (Opera House) that was constructed by Paul Chevenard in 1831 on the site of town hall's old gardens. It is square in shape with a row of columns on top of which are decorative plinths and eight of

The Palais du Commerce, which acts as stock exchange, commercial court, and stockbroking headquarters, dates from the Second Empire (1852–1870).

the nine muses, there not being any space left for the ninth, Urania, the muse of astronomy. It was given a new look in 1993 by Jean Nouvel, who gave it an enormous glass dome, and reconstructed the entire interior, except for the foyer, decorating it in black.

Opposite is the rear entrance of the Hôtel de Ville (town hall), which can be better appreciated by going to the Place des Terreaux by way of the Rue Joseph Serlin. This large square was created in the 17th century on the site of former marshland. The Bartholdi fountain, which was originally erected in 1894 on the square's west side, was moved in 1994 due to the installation by Christian Drevet and Daniel Buren of 69 illuminated fountains of varying height and intensity.

The Hôtel de Ville was built by the city's chief highways engineer, Simon Maupin, helped by the mathematician,

The construction of the Hôtel de Ville (town hall) lasted from 1646 to 1672. It has since been the subject of a great many alterations, both to its exterior and to its interior.

Girard Desargues, and the painters, Germain Panthot and Thomas Blanchet, between 1646 and 1672. The upper parts of the building were destroyed by fire in 1674, and reconstruction work to plans by Jules Hardouin-Mansart and Robert de Cotte began in 1701. Alterations were carried out on the exterior sculpted decoration during the mid-19th century, and to the interior during the Second Empire. The rather narrow main front is made up of a first floor and an attic, which in this case is the portion of the wall above the main cornice, above a ground floor. The domed corner buildings are decorated with pediments depicting the cardinal virtues of courage, justice, prudence, and temperance. Four bronze medallions made by Fabisch in 1855 feature Louis XIII, Anne of Austria, Louis XIV, and Henry IV, as portrayed in the engravings of Claude Warin. An 1829 statue of Henry IV by Legendre-Héral, has replaced that of his grandson, Louis XIV, by Chabry, which was pulled down in 1792. The entrance porch is framed by porphyry columns, while a belfry with a set of 40 bells stands over the whole building. The side wings are long and frame the main courtyard, which is reached from the entrance hall and which ends in a row of columns. It is here that summer concerts take place and where a dinner for the G7 summit was held. There then follows the lower courtyard, which has lost its gardens. Inside, the walls of the main staircase, which starts in the foyer, are painted with a scene depicting 'The fire of Lugdunum in the time of Nero in 65 A.D.', while 'The triumph of the city' decorates the ceiling. The 17th century ceilings have been preserved in the Napoleon III rooms, with 'The glory of Louis XIV' in the Salle de la Nomination, 'The greatness of Lyons during the Consulate (1799–1804)' in the Salle du Consulat, and 'The fall of the vices' in the Salle de la Conservation.

The Hôtel de Ville's main courtyard is the venue for summer concerts.

The square's southern side is filled by the large complex of buildings that is the Palais Saint-Pierre, which was originally the convent of the Dames de Saint-Pierre, and which is now the Musée de Beaux Arts (Art Gallery). It was possibly founded in the time of the Merovingians, but there is clear evidence of its existence during the Carolingian period, when the rules of the Benedictine Order were adopted, and it was reconstructed in the late 12th and 13th centuries. In the Rue Paul Chevenard can be seen the tower's doorway, which is a late Romanesque porch where two archivolts carved with foliage and animals' heads are supported by small columns. The convent was finally demolished in the 17th century, but was reconstructed between 1659 and 1686 by François de Royers de la Valfenière and his son, Paul, who were architects from Avignon. After the nuns left the convent during the Revolution, it was used for a variety of purposes until Napoleon made it a museum in 1803. The palace is entered by a pleasant garden surrounded by a cloister and filled with statues of birds, and is a place in which the noise of the city centre are soon forgotten. The large main staircase, which was designed by Thomas Blanchet, and the refectory, which is a lovely Baroque room with its stucco figures and paintings by Pierre-Louis Cretey, are evidence of the convent's wealth. The museum is the work of René Dardel (1832-1850), Abraham Hirsch (1875-1888), Jean-Gabriel

The Musée des Beaux-Art's superb collections.

Mortamet, Philippe Dubois, and Jean-Michel Vilmotte (1990-1998). Conceived to be as comprehensive as possible in scope, the museum is divided into five extensive collections of antiquities, 'objets d'art', paintings, sculptures, and graphic art, which are housed in 70 rooms. It was well endowed with objects during the Napoleonic period, and has since purchased or been donated many extremely interesting pieces, the most recent of which being the Jacqueline Delubac donation, among which paintings, and particularly 19th century French paintings, predominate. Its nickname of the 'little Louvre' is therefore well-deserved.

The west side of the square is occupied by a handsome 19th century building that houses the Galerie des Terreaux, which is unfortunately closed, while on the north

The Napoléon III rooms in the Hôtel de Ville.

In summer, the north side of the Place Terreaux swarms with lots of pavement cafés.

The church of Saint-Nizier is a Gothic building.

side, the many cafés set out their tables and parasols for their customers in summer. The construction under the square of an underground car park enabled excavations to be carried out on the medieval walls, during which everyday objects were unearthed. Matt Mullican has engraved images of Lyons on the car park's floor.

Turn left out of the Palais Saint-Pierre into the Rue de Constantine where lovely blocks of flats were built in the 19th century in the old butchers' district of the Terreaux, which lay between the Rue d'Algérie and the Rue d'Oran. This street leads to the very attractive Quai de la Pêcherie where you can stroll while pausing to leaf through the books on the second-hand book stalls right opposite Old Lyons. There is a food market every

The Rue Mercière is a focus
for fashionable restaurants.

day except Monday on the Quai Saint-Antoine, which follows on from the Quai de la Pêcherie down the riverside.

Turn into the Place d'Albon, which used to be at one end of the only bridge over the Saône, and then into the Rue des Bouquetiers and the Place Saint-Nizier, where the Gothic church of the same name stands. It is not outside the realms of possibility that its site corresponds with that of the church and burial place built in the 5th century on the graves of the martyrs of 177, and where Bishop Nizier was buried in 573. This early church was repaired several times during the centuries that followed, and was finally completely rebuilt in the 14th century. Several alterations were carried out between the 15th and 18th centuries to both the interior and exterior, some of which can clearly be seen on the west front. The north tower and its steeple of pink brick dates from the 15th century, while the Renaissance central porch, consisting of a coffered semi-dome resting on columns, is the work of Jean Vallet, and not of Philippe Delorme. The neo-Flamboyant south tower with its openwork design is 19th century in date. The church's interior is simple, with a central nave and two side

aisles onto which open some chapels. The first chapel is covered by a high vaulted ceiling of virtually flat ribbing, whereas the others have sexpartite vaulting. A very elaborately decorated triforium runs above the large arcades. The statue of Notre-Dame-des-Grâces by Antoine Coysevox and the bas-reliefs of the Assumption by Mimerel are from the 17th century, the high altar from the 18th century, and the organ, the wood panelling, the stained glass windows, and the other altars from the 19th century. Shops are built right up to the church's walls, especially in the Rue de la Fromagerie.

The Rue de la Poulaillerie is to be found two streets further down, and at number 13, the former Hôtel de la Couronne, a typical medieval Lyons house, was used as a town hall in the early 17th century. Since 1964, the city council, who had been given it by Crédit Lyonnaise, have made part of it into the Musée de la Banque (Banking Museum), and most of it into the Musée de l'Imprimerie (Printing Museum), which is one of the most important in Europe. It is not content simply to exhibit incunabula (early printed books, especially those printed before 1501), woodcuts, litho-

The Musée de la Banque et de l'Imprimerie (Banking and Printing Museum) is housed in the old town hall.

Middle Ages to 1830, was the main thoroughfare of the city between the Pont du Change and the Pont de la Guillotière. A whole variety of activities filled the area, with weapons, spices, cloth, and metals sold by the Germans and Swiss in the north, haberdashers and sellers of furnishing trimmings in the centre, and printers and bookshops in the south. Although the area escaped demolition, it became increasingly run down, turning into a red-light district. However, the same area today has been extremely well restored, and is full of fashionable restaurants which in summer overflow onto the pavements. Among other restored houses, that of Horace Cardon, which was built in 1550, stands at number 68. At number 56, the Passage Mercière leads to the Quai Saint-Antoine, and at number 30 is the old commandery of the Antonins, where those suffering from the gangrenous form of ergotism, an illness caused by a fungal disease of cereals, and especially of rye, were cared for, and whose pigs were allowed to run free in the city. On the first floor can still be seen the front door of the old Guignol theatre, which has since become the home of the Théâtre des Ateliers.

The Rue Mercière opens into the Rue de Brest where, just opposite, is the Passage de l'Argue, which was built in 1825 with a glass roof, and which is the only one to have survived among the many that Lyons used to have. The Place des Jacobins bears the name of the Dominican monks whose monastery used to stand there. The Order was dissolved in 1790, and the monastery buildings housed the Prefecture until the Second Empire, whilst the church, which contained many 16th century tombs of rich Florentines, was demolished in 1823. The square is now the junction of three streets constructed between 1840 and 1856, and the fountain in the middle is dedicated to four of Lyons' artistic celebrities, the architect, Philibert Delorme, the engraver, Gérard Audran, the sculptor, Guillaume Coustou, and the painter, Hippolyte Flandrin.

Take the Rue Fabre to the Place des Célestins, whose name is a reminder that the site was occupied by this particular religious order before its dissolution in 1773. The destruction of the religious buildings enabled a new district to be opened up, which included the construction of a theatre, that was demolished in 1871, but which was followed by the construction, in a mixture of styles, of the present theatre on the same site by Gaspard André, helped by the sculptor, Roubaud, and the painter, Domer. The small square in front of the theatre conceals an arca-

graphs, and other rare items, such as the 'placards contre le messe' (proclamations against the mass) of 1534, but also displays tools, printing presses, and a working printer's workshop.

Cross the Rue de Brest by the Rue Dubois to get to the Rue Mercière (the Roman 'Via Mercatoria') which, from the

The Bartholdi Fountain

This was not intended for Lyons at all, but for Bordeaux, as it was meant to represent the rivers Garonne and Dordogne flowing together to reach the Atlantic Ocean. Bordeaux did not follow up its order, and so Lyons City Council bought it, reinterpreting its subject to be that of the marriage of the rivers Saône and the Rhône.

Street names in the Mercière district

The commercial nature of the district is much in evidence. Apart from the Rue Mercière (haberdasher) itself, there are the Rues de la Fromagerie (cheese), de la Poulaillerie (poultry), and de la Grenette (grain), and the Quai de la Pêcherie where cheese, poultry, grain, and fish could be bought. In the Rue Tupin and Rue Dubois could be bought pots and wood, and to brighten up your house or your wife, you went to the Rue des Bouquetiers (flowers). By means of these names, the distribution of trades can be found in the specialist areas so characteristic of medieval and early modern towns. The district also has some beautiful shops whose décor has never been touched since they were first built, e.g. the 'cuirs et peaux' (leather) shop at 15, rue Tupin, the Quincaillerie Rode (ironmonger) at 14, rue Confort, and the Café des Négociants at the corner of the Rue Herriot and Rue Grenette.

Edouard Herriot (this latter being the former Rue de l'Impératrice) which are full of elegant shops, or the Rue de la République via the Rue des Archers, where the headquarters of Lyons' Company of Archers used to be situated. In this part of the 'Rue de Ré', at number 79, is the Pathé cinema dating from 1933, at number 85, the old 1877 Kursaal casino with its caryatid-decorated balcony, and which used to be the headquarters of the 'Le Progrès' newspaper, before becoming that of FNAC, while, at number 4, place de la Visite, is an Art Deco building.

The Place des Jacobins is named after the Dominicans whose monastery stood here until 1790.

Underneath the Place des Célestins is a spiral arcaded underground car park which was designed by Michel Targe, and which can be looked at thanks to Daniel Buren's 'Periscope'.

ded spiral underground car park designed by Michel Targe, which can be observed with the aid of a periscope designed by Daniel Buren, that is equipped, deep-down, with a giant revolving mirror.

The Place Bellecour can be rejoined by way of the Quai des Célestins, which has good views of the footbridge to the Palais de Justice (Law Courts), built by Delfante and Lamboley in 1984, Fourvière, the archway that used to be the entrance to the Célestins' monastery near the Place Antoine Gourju, and the 17th century former Hôtel Perrachon at number 1, rue Colonel Chambonnet. On the other hand, you may prefer to take the Rues Emile Zola, Gasparin, and

Croix-Rousse

CHAPTER 5

Clinging to its hillside that rises up between the Rhône and Saône, Croix-Rousse is one of the most typical and most attractive parts of Lyons. It remains deeply influenced by the poignant history of the silk-workers who came to live here in the 19th century, and has preserved its working-class soul which still exists in its cafés, 'boules' pitches, and market. However, it must be made clear exactly which Croix-Rousse is being talked about, the slopes or the plateau. This distinction is historic, as in the 16th century the two parts were separated by walls with three gates, with Lyons lying on the side of the slopes, whilst on the plateau side lay the land which belonged to the Seigneur de Cuire until the siege of Lyons in 1793, and which was an indication of Croix-Rousse's independence. All this ended in 1852 when Croix-Rousse, Vaise, and La Guillotière became integral parts of Lyons. Today, the district has become very trendy, with property developers fighting over the smallest free square metre, new blocks of flats sprouting up like mushrooms, and the sale prices of flats rising continuously. However it only takes a short stroll through the streets to feel once more the spirit of Croix-Rousse that is felt so very quickly by newcomers.

The climbs up the streets in Croix-Rousse are often tough-going, so the least tiring way of exploring the area without getting too much out of breath is to follow the reverse of the chronological order. The town's development actually started at the foot of the slopes and gra-

dually worked its way up to the top, so the tour begins on the plateau and works its way down to the Place des Terreaux. The starting-point is the Place de la Croix-Rousse, which is served by both bus and metro links.

In Croix-Rousse, it is far better to go down the hill rather than go up it given the steepness of the slope! This is the Montée de Vauzelle.

Opposite:
Colourful buildings in Croix-Rousse.

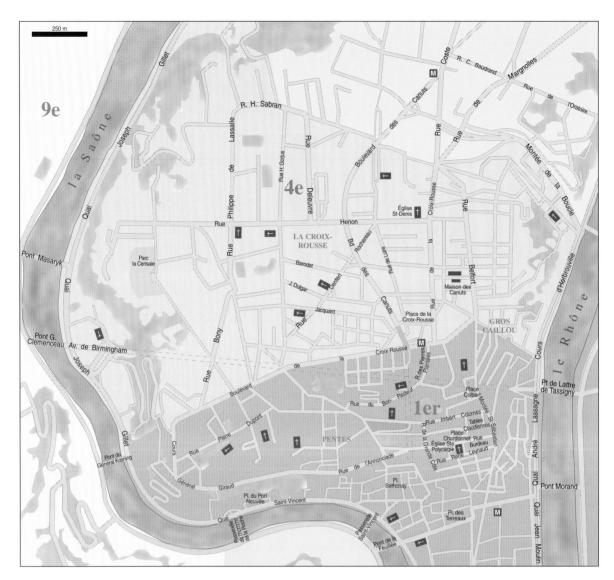

250 m

9e

R. H. Sabran

la Saône

Joseph

Quai

Lassalle

Rue

de

Philippe

4e

Delewre

Rue H. Gorjus

Rue

Rue

Boulevard

des

Canuts

Coste

M

R. C. Baudrand

Margnolles

Rue

de

l'Oratoire

Montée de la Boucle

Église
St-Denis

Rue

Croix-Rousse

la

de

Rue

LA CROIX-
ROUSSE

Henon

Bd.

Rochetaile

Rue de la rue

de

Belfort

Maison des
Canuts

GROS
CAILLOU

d'Herbrouville

le Rhône

Pont Masaryk

Quai

Parc
la Cerisaie

Barodet

J. Dulgar

Danfert

Jacquard

Rue

des

Canuts

Rue

Place de la
Croix-Rousse

Cours

Pont G.
Clémenceau

Av. de Birmingham

Pont du
Général Koening

Rue

Bony

Joseph

Boulevard

de

la

Croix-Rousse

M

R. des Pierres
Plantées

1er

Pt de Lattre
de Tassigny

Gillet

Cours

Rue

Pierre

Dupont

Rue du   Bon- Pasteur

PENTES

Rue de   l'Annonciade

Rue Imbert
Colomes
Tables
Claudiennes

Place
Colbert

Montée St-Sébastien

Lassagne

André

Pt de Lattre
de Tassigny

Place
Chardonnet
Église Ste
Polycarpe

Rue

Rue

Bordeau

René   Leynaud

Quai

Jean- Moulin

Pont Morand

Général

Giraud

Pl. du Port
Neuville

Saint-Vincent

Pl.
Sathonay

Pl. des
Terreaux

M

Quai

Passerelle
de la Roche

Quai

Passerelle
Saint-Vincent

Pont de
la Feuillée

From the thread woven by a craftsman at the Maison des Canuts (Silk Workers Centre) to the piece of silk: a living tradition.

THE PLATEAU

Croix-Rousse's name comes from the cross carved from Couzon stone, which today is called 'golden stone' because of its colour, that was erected in the area in the 16th century, almost certainly on the present Place Joannès Ambre, which lies at the end of the Grande Rue de la Croix-Rousse before reaching Caluire. Although it had long been a market gardening area, very few people lived in Croix-Rousse at that time. On the access roads, the most important of which was the Grande Rue de la Croix-Rousse, there were some coaching inns and wine merchants, who took advantage of the traffic between Lyons and north-east France. Construction in the area increased during the 17th century, but it was not until the 19th century and the arrival of the silk-workers that the urbanisation process really began.

GRANDE RUE DE LA CROIX-ROUSSE

The visit to the Plateau begins symbolically with the statue of **Jacquard** which stands in the middle of the Place de la Croix-Rousse. From 1804 onwards, this Lyons mechanical engineer (1752–1834) perfected the first loom that enabled several warp threads to be selected at the same time thanks to a system of perforated cards, with only one workman being needed to operate it. This technical revolution forced the silk-workers to leave their homes in Saint-Georges to come to live in Croix-Rousse so as to house the looms in flats of a suitable height.

Behind the square starts the Grande Rue de la Croix-Rousse, one of the most important and oldest streets in the area. Walk to the junction with the Rue d'Ivry and then turn right. At number 10 can be heard the sound of 'bistanclaque', the written transcription of the noise made by a loom, at the **Maison des Canuts** (House of the Silk-workers), where craftsmen explain weaving techniques

and the working of the different looms which succeeded each other over the centuries, as well as selling their creations in the shop directly opposite. On coming out of the Maison des Canuts, carry on along the Grande Rue de la Croix-Rousse, where, here and there, e.g. at numbers 13, 49, and 55, and opposite at numbers 52 and 58/62, are small single or two-storied houses that were built during the 17th and 18th centuries and are reminders of a Croix-Rousse which was then still mainly rural. At

Jacquard's statue, one of the area's many symbols, in the Place de la Croix-Rousse.

True or false? The 'Mur des Canuts' (Silk-Workers' Wall) is a giant 'trompe-l'oeil' mural.

The Rosa Mir garden: a tangled mass of stones and shells.

number 40, the carriage entrance marks the entry to an old coaching inn which has preserved its wooden gallery. At number 77 stands the **Cinéma Saint-Denis.** It was in 1922 that this former parish hall showed its first film on a white sheet stretched out in the yard of Saint-Denis' school, and since the end of the Second World War, it has enjoyed voluntary organisation status, its distinctive feature being that it is run by volunteers. The cinema has retained its former character, despite the fact that it has been regularly refurbished, and today can welcome 237 cinema-goers, including 37 in the balcony. Nearby on the same side of the road, at number 83, a Spanish mason, Jules Sénis, has constructed a curious garden of stones and shells to which he has given the name of his mother, **Rosa Mir.** Go up the Grande Rue de la Croix-Rousse and turn right into the Rue Hénon. After the 17th century church of Saint-Denis, which underwent alterations in the 19th century, is to be found one of the entrances to Croix-Rousse hospital, which was opened in 1861. Turn left onto the Boulevard des Canuts, where, at the corner of the Rue Denfert-Rochereau, the 'Mur des Canuts' (Wall of the Silk-workers) is impossible to miss as it is a giant mural of 1,200 m², conceived as a 'trompe-l'oeil' by the Cité de la Création studio in 1987. Ten years later, the artists are at work again, in order to take into account the changes in the area, with, on the right, a new and rather up-market building that has replaced the old silk-workers' building. Carry on to the Boulevard de la Croix-Rousse, then turn left, passing once again the Place de la Croix-Rousse.

The Silk-Workers' Revolts

Lyons' history is closely interlinked with that of silk. From 1540 onwards, the city had the monopoly of the market in silk, and was thus the only authorised general entrepôt in the kingdom of France. The industry prospered until the Revolution, with almost 60,000 people employed in it, but unemployment and falling prices after the Revolution lead to increasing poverty in many families. The silk-workers very rapidly made their opposition known to the silk-manufacturers, and in 1831, they demanded a minimum rate, which they eventually got from the prefect, Bouvier-Dumolard. However, most of the silk-manufacturers took no notice of this, and a first revolt started on 21 November. The arrival of troops stopped it within a few days, but three years later, in April, 1834, the silk-workers returned to the streets to protest against the fall in jobbing work. However, the army dislodged them from their barricades within six days. From these two bloody revolts was born a real sense of class struggle and solidarity, exemplified by the creation of the first friendly societies, and symbolised by the silk-workers' famous slogan of 'Vivre en travaillant ou mourir en combattant' (Live working or die fighting).

BOULEVARD DE LA CROIX-ROUSSE

At the eastern end of the boulevard sits the **Gros Caillou** (Big Stone), an erratic boulder from the time of the Ice Age, that was found in 1890 when the Tunnel de la Ficelle linking the Presqu'île to the plateau was being built. Legend tells how this large stone is actually the heart of a bailiff who wanted to turn a whole family of silk-workers out onto the street. In order to punish him, God turned his heart into stone, took it out of his body, and forced the bailiff to push it along until he met someone who was nastier than him... hence the stone's large size!

Below the Gros Caillou, the Place Bellevue enjoys a superb view of Lyons' left bank, and from here, there is direct access to the quays on the banks of the Rhône by way of the staircase of the Montée du Boulevard, which runs alongside the walls of the old Fort Saint-Laurent. This formed part of the fortifications in Lyons that were built in 1830, only to be demolished 35 years later to make way for the extension of the Boulevard de la Croix-Rousse.

With the Gros Caillou behind you, return to the Place de la Croix-Rousse. Take the Rue Aimé Boussange on the right, at the Post Office corner, and push open the sliding gate which stands halfway up the street, just after the Post Office. At the bottom of the courtyard is the old Porte Saint-Sébastien which used to mark the entrance into Lyons. Go back to the Place de la Croix-Rousse.

The wide plane-tree-lined **Boulevard de la Croix-Rousse** has the pretentious appearance typical of Second Empire town planning, and its construction involved the demolition of the old fortifications that used to separate Lyons from the former independent town of Croix-Rousse. One of the best food markets in Lyons is held here from Tuesday to Sunday on the northern side of the street, and in addition, there are market stalls every Tuesday that sell materials and clothing on the other side of the road. The 19th century front of the town hall can be seen further down the boulevard.

The 'Gros Caillou' (Big Stone): this boulder, which was carried here during the Ice Age, is, according to the legend linked to it, a genuine symbol of the silk workers' district.

The Boulevard de la Croix-Rousse is a beautiful major thoroughfare that dates from the Second Empire.

The drapes and gilding of the baldaquin in the beautiful Baroque church of Saint-Bruno give it an impressive appearance.

A little lower down on the other side of the road, the present Institut Universitaire de Formation des Maîtres (University Department for Teacher Training) has preserved the former main gate of the 17th century Château de la Tourette. Carry on along the boulevard up to the Rue Leroudier which then cuts across the rue Pierre Dupont. The majestic church of **Saint-Bruno**, whose octagonal dome can be seen for miles, is the former monastery church of the Carthusians, the order founded by St Bruno in 1084. Its architecture is Baroque in style, being constructed during the 17th and 18th centuries, with the architect, Soufflot, contributing to its design. The only exception to this is the west front, which was completed in the late 19th century. Inside, an impressive canopy made of painted and gilded cloth and plaster hangs over the altar.

Almost opposite the church of Saint-Bruno, at the other side of the boulevard, is the biggest park in the area, La Cerisaie (Cherry Orchard). The people of

It is a real pleasure to stroll around Saint-Croix market – held every day except Monday.

Croix-Rousse love to take the air in what used to be the property of a family of chemists and silk-manufacturers, the Gillets, whose house is now the centre for a variety of cultural organisations. Go along the boulevard as far as the Cours Général Giraud, from where there is an absolutely beautiful view of Fourvière's leafy hill just opposite.

THE SLOPES

Because it has been so deeply influenced by the history of the silk-workers, this district has tended to forget its

Silk-workers' flats in Croix-Rousse

In comparison with the houses in Old Lyons, these tall and very plain buildings can seem very poverty-stricken, but they were constructed with one purely functional objective in mind, that of housing the silk-workers and their new Jacquard looms, which took up a lot of space. The architects had to incorporate several essential features. There had to be good high ceilings of a minimum height of 3.90 metres, large windows to let in the maximum amount of sunlight, and alleys under the buildings, covered if possible, to enable passage through the area from one street to another by using the 'traboules'. All the flats have the same lay-out, with the loom occupying most of the lower room, and the family sleeping on the mezzanine floor.

Roman past when it was called Condate and when delegates from the Three Gauls filled its amphitheatre at the beginning of the Christian era. In the 17th century, its slopes were covered with monasteries and convents, but during the French Revolution, the Church's properties were sold off, and in their place were built the first silk-workers' flats, which are much sought-after today because of their high beamed ceilings.

The area has been designated as a 'Zone de Protection du Patrimoine' (Conservation Area) since 1994, and the part belonging to the 1st 'arrondissement' has been listed by Unesco as a World Heritage Site, so the most difficult thing to do is to choose a route because the possibilities are endless. Chronologically, a visit should begin half-way up the slope, in front of the amphitheatre of the Three Gauls, but to obtain a better flavour of the district, it is better to 'tear down' the hillside using the 'traboules', just as the 19th century silk-workers did. The area's most prominent buildings can be seen with a few short detours from this route.

It took three hundred years to completely finish the building of the church of Saint-Bruno.

62

MONTÉE DE LA GRANDE-CÔTE

Before beginning the trip around the 'traboules', go to the Rue des Pierres-Plantées, at the top of the Boulevard de la Croix-Rousse. At the end of this short, sloping street a viewing point has been laid out and enlarged, and this gives superb sweeping views of Old Lyons and the quays of the Saône, as well as of the church-topped Fourvière Hill. This is the starting-point for the Montée de la Grande-Côte, the 800 metre-long street which boldly climbs along what was for centuries the main thoroughfare between Lyons and the former suburb of Croix-Rousse. A series of demolitions have seriously scarred this attractive 'montée', but there still remain some beautiful buildings that bear witness to the 16th and 17th centuries. There is, for example, the lovely house at number 63 at the corner of the Rue des Tables-Claudiennes, a spiral staircase in the driveway at number 67, restored house fronts between numbers 98 and 108, and a building constructed of golden stone at number 116. Today, the Montée de la Grande-Côte is an integral part of the Unesco-listed site, and its restoration is now in progress. The architect, Alain Marguerit, and other landscape architects have refurbished the upper part to make pleasant terraces.

A WALK AROUND THE 'TRABOULES'

Sometimes in the form of courtyards, sometimes in the form of steps down alleyways, these passages linking two streets, whose name comes from the Latin 'trans ambulare' or 'to walk across', enabled the silk-workers to take their bundles of silk more quickly down to the manufacturers right at the bottom of the hill. These short-cuts through the streets and the use of covered passageways meant that their precious cargo was protected from bad weather. The walk begins at the Boulevard de la Croix-Rousse. Go down the Montée Saint-Sébastien to the Place Colbert which stands to the right of it, taking the Rue du Général de Sève just after the imposing church of Saint-Bernard, built in 1866. Right at the bottom of this pretty, shady square, at number 9, is the Cour des Voraces, the most famous and the most popular 'traboule' in Croix-Rousse. Its 19th century monumental staircase with its flight of very steep steps and solid pillars is today a listed historical monument on the Inventaire des Monuments Historiques, and this comes as no surprise. It used to be the meeting place of a silk-workers' organisation, the Voraces, who took part in the 1848 Revolution by creating armed militias.

There is a superb view of Lyons from the Montée Saint-Sébastien.

Croix-Rousse seen from above: tiled roofs and long frontages.

An interplay of silk and lighting effects in the Cour de Voraces for the festival of lights on 8 December.

From the courtyard, go under the staircase to come out onto a narrow street, from where the 'traboule' lies to the right. Another staircase, a new courtyard, and then number 29, rue Imbert Colomès is reached. Just opposite, at number 20, is another 'traboule' that leads to the Rue des Tables-Claudiennes, so called because it was here that part of a speech given by the Emperor Claudius in 48 A.D. was found engraved on a piece of bronze. The Roman emperor, who was born in Lyons, was addressing members of the Roman senate and asking them to accept Gaul's dignitaries as senators.

To the right is the Place Chardonnet, one of the lovely shady squares which make Croix-Rousse so attractive.

An extremely original staircase in the Cour des Voraces.

Chestnut trees and solid silk workers' buildings in the peaceful Place Chardonnet.

AMPHITHEATRE
OF THE THREE GAULS

Below, the Rue Burdeau leads to the Amphitheatre of the Three Gauls (to the right when leaving the square). This was built by Caius Rufus in 19 A.D., then enlarged 100 years later to accommodate 20,000 spectators, and is the site, every year, of a gathering of delegates from 60 cities of the Three Gauls, i.e. from the former Celtic Gaul, Belgian Gaul, and Aquitaine. Gladiator fights and public speaking competitions were both held here, but the most harrowing event that ever took place in the amphitheatre was the martyrdom of the first Christians, including St Blandine, in 177 A.D., an event that is commemorated today by a wooden post standing in the arena. To the left of the amphitheatre, the former 19th century botanical garden, which has now been moved to the Parc de la Tête-d'Or (see the section on the Right Bank), has been replaced by a lawned area with a view of the pretty Place Sathonay.

The site of the amphitheatre of the Three Gauls, which was constructed in 19 A.D.

The Place Sathonay – an oasis of coolness much appreciated by boules players.

A WALK AROUND THE 'TRABOULES' (CONTINUED)

The Rue Burdeau, which runs alongside the Place Chardonnet, leads to the Passage Mermet (number 34, on the left-hand pavement), but even better is the Passage Thiaffait (numbers 30 and 30 bis)and its double flight of stairs that lead to a beautiful courtyard which has been completely restored. During the last two years, a variety of designers have set up shop here, and are trying to bring back life to a street which for a long time was in a deplorable state. The Passages Mermet and Thiaffait both lead directly to the Rue René Leynaud.

The Maison Brunet's impressive façade has 365 windows.

CHURCH OF SAINT-POLYCARPE AND THE CONDITIONS DES SOIES

At 25, rue René Leynaud, you need to step back a bit in order to admire the impressive church of Saint-Polycarpe, founded in the 17th century by the Oratorians in the monastery and convent district. The west front was designed a century later by one of Soufflot's pupils, and contrasts sharply with the other buildings in the street because of its ornamentation and the whiteness of its stone. Then go down to the small, circular Place Forez, which leads to the **Conditions de Soie** at 7, rue Saint-

Polycarpe. This beautiful Tuscan-style building was constructed in 1814 by the architect, Joseph Jean Gay. Its warehouses and laboratories were used for the valuation of silk, the calculation of its moisture content, and the judging of its quality before establishing a price. Mulberry leaves and silkworms carved on the doorway are evidence of the building's former function. After the fall of the silk industry due to the fatal blow dealt to it by the discovery of new synthetic fibres, the Condition des Soies fell into disuse, but is now a flourishing social and cultural centre.

A WALK AROUND
THE 'TRABOULES' (END)

The walk around the 'traboules' continues at number 6, rue René Leynaud, which joins up with number 5, rue des Capucins. By number 6, rue des Capucins, just a little bit higher up on the other side of the street, there is direct access to the Place des Capucins by taking the steps in the courtyard. A new, recently restored staircase leads directly down to the Place des Terreaux, but in order to finish this walk among beautiful surroundings, take the Rue Sainte-Catherine to the left and then the 'traboule' at number 12 up to the Place des Terreaux. A lion's head, that of the Bartholdi Fountain in the Place des Terreaux, is framed to perfection in the view down the alley, right to the very end.

MAISON BRUNET
MAISON DES 365 FENÊTRES

Croix-Rousse cannot be left without seeing the 'House with 365 Windows'. From the Place des Terreaux, go down to the Quai Saint-Vincent by way of the Rue Algérie. To the right is the district of La Martinière to where a quick visit can be made to see the old La Martinière's girls' school, which has some beautiful mosaics, at 33, rue de la Martinière, and the Salle Rameau, at number 29, which were both built in the early 20th century. Go back to the Quai Saint-Vincent, glancing at the mural on the corner. This is the 'fresque des Lyonnais' (people of Lyons' fresco), another Cité de la Création designed 'trompe-l'oeil', which groups together about thirty of Lyons' famous personalities, from the Emperor Claudius to Bertrand Tavernier, the film director.

With your back to the Saône, the full length of the Maison des 365 Fenêtres can easily be seen on the hillside. It stands at numbers 5 and 6, place Rouville, between the Cours Général Giraud and the Rue de l'Annonciade, and was built by the architect, Brunet, who was extremely interested in cosmology. His plans were governed by a strong symbolic system with 365 windows (number of days in a year), 6 floors (days in the week, less Sunday), 52 rooms (weeks), and 4 entrances (seasons). The silk-workers took refuge here during the 1831 revolt so as to return fire at the army that was positioned lower down. At the foot of the Maison Brunet, the Chartreux garden offers a pleasant way down to the quays.

Vogue
des Marrons
(Chestnut Fair)

Every year for almost 200 years, the Croix-Rousse plateau has hummed to the sound of roundabouts and been bathed in the scent of candyfloss and roast chestnuts. In the past, the fair used to take place all year round in several streets and squares in the area, but now it is only in the Boulevard de la Croix-Rousse that stallholders come for four weeks during the chestnut season, from the October half-term holidays to mid-November.

Vaise, la Duchère, and Île Barbe

CHAPTER 6

The Vaise area of Lyons, which lies on the banks of the Saône, used to be a very fertile plain during the Middle Ages. Industrial development took place in the 19th century with the establishment of a large number of factories and warehouses, and now further plans promoting residential and high technology development have been pushing forward over several years. The 'village' aspect of this former suburb, which became part of Lyons in 1852, has, nevertheless, not been forgotten, despite the ever-increasing number of blocks of flats. The arrival of businesses specialising in the new technologies, e.g. video games and computer software, should give a fresh boost to the old industrial wasteland in the dockland area by the side of the Saône, from the Quai du Commerce to the Quai Paul Sédallian.

A visit to Vaise begins at the Place de Paris, at the terminus of line D of the metro, 'Gare de Vaise' station.

The church of the Annunciation, built by the architect, Paul Koch, stands in the middle of the square. Its steeple is particularly eye-catching because, just like a mobile, the cross-shaped steeple is surrounded at its base by little copper angels that glitter in the sunshine.

Next, walk along the Rue Masaryk to the Quai Jaÿr, where there view of the lovely 19th century suspension bridge that spans the Saône in a rather jaunty fashion.

Right from the striking metro station at Valmy (far left) to the Gorges-du-Loup business district (left), Vaise is most resolutely modern in appearance.

The interplay of light and speed in the 'Gare de Vaise' metro station.

HIGH-RISE FLATS AT 24, QUAI JAŸR

In 1910, Emmanuel Cateland built Lyons' first 'skyscraper', made entirely of reinforced concrete, at the corner of the Quai Jaÿr and the Rue Saint-Cyr. A frieze of graphic designs in blue mosaic adds a touch of discreet decoration to the front of the building at mezzanine floor level.

Vaise railway station.

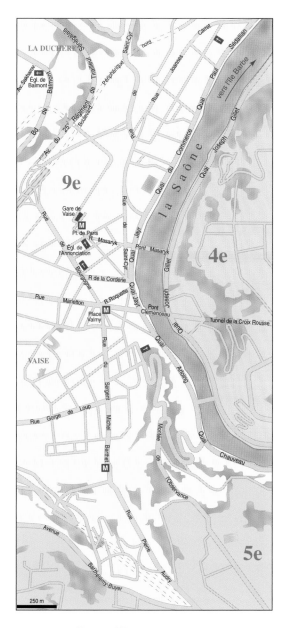

Lyons along the river

From April to the end of October, boats offering picturesque commentated cruises that last about an hour sail along the rivers Saône and Rhône, taking in the Île Barbe, the banks of the Saône from Saint-Georges to Vaise, and the confluence of the Saône and Rhône, opposite the old Palais de Justice. More romantic is the 'Illuminations' trip, which gives a good impression of Lyons' 'Plan Lumière' (Lighting Plan), by which many of its buildings, bridges, and quays are floodlit. This particular boat trip is only available on Saturday evenings at 9.30pm, from 7 July to 25 August.

Lyons can be discovered on its rivers during spring and summer.

PLACE VALMY

From the roundabout, take the Rue Roquette which leads straight to the Place Valmy, the traditional heart of Vaise and the starting point of the area's busy shopping streets, the Rue Marietton, Rue de Bourgogne, and Grande Rue de Vaise. The square was completely restored with the arrival of the metro, and is now also the site of the new Vaise 'médiathèque' (multi-media library), which is a glass and metal structure designed by the architects, Godivier and Vella.

LA DUCHÈRE

The La Duchère plateau with its immense concrete blocks of flats blots out the horizon on the hills above Vaise. This housing development was designed during the 1950s by the architects, Cottin and Grimal, and is made up of the areas of Le Château, Le Plateau, Balmont, and La Sauvegarde, all of which extend over an area of 600 hectares from the edge of Vaise. Nothing now remains of the old 17th château of La Duchère, but the 19th century fort at Balmont, which encircles the area's

71

Vaise's multi-media resource centre is a recent example of modern architecture.

Church of Notre-Dame-de-la-Duchère and a Tour of the Plateau

Continue right onto the Avenue Sakharov and then turn left onto the Avenue du Plateau. Just behind the impressive 100 metre-high tower-block with triangular-shaped balconies is concealed the church of Notre-Dame-de-la-Duchère, which is half-buried in the ground under a grassy mound. It was designed by Cottin in 1969, and is a good example of original modern architecture with its glass walls and a pagoda-shaped roof.

Île Barbe

From the plateau of La Duchère, go back down to Vaise via the Boulevard de la Duchère and take the quays in the direction of Saint-Cyr-au-Mont-d'Or. At the end of the Quai Paul Sédaillian, the Saône suddenly branches into two to give way to a small bank of earth shaped like a ship's hull and over which stands a beautiful Romanesque tower. This is the Île Barbe. This rocky 'île barbare' (barbarian island), covered with dense foliage, was the site of a powerful abbey from Merovingian times, with about 100 monks living there during the Carolingian period. It passed under secular management in the mid-16th century, was seriously damaged by the Protestants later on in the 16th century during the Wars of Religion, and finally fell into oblivion after being sold after the French Revolution. Today, some architectural evidence of the abbey and its outbuildings can still be found in the walls of private houses. Lost under all the vegetation are beautiful buildings which still have mullioned windows (in the narrow central street, right after the car park and the Place Notre-Dame), arches, and a Romanesque doorway (Impasse Saint-Louis, behind the restaurant – which is excellent, by the way – to the left after the car park). The pleasantest way of visiting the Île-Barbe is to simply stroll along, soaking up the island's romantic atmosphere. A free car park on the mainland, with access to the island via the Pont de l'Île Barbe, enables visitors to leave their cars very near the entrance, and also to enjoy, at the same time, the sight of the 'boules' players who come to play here on the shady terrace. Before returning to the

sports centre, is still clearly visible, and this is the starting-point for the visit. Take the car up here from Vaise via the Rue de Bourgogne or Rue Marietton.

Musée des Sapeurs-Pompiers (Fire Services Museum)

France's largest museum dedicated to the fire services stands behind the firemen's barracks in the far west of Belmont. From the first force pumps, the earliest of which in the museum dates from 1740, to the latest state-of-the-art diving suits, all aspects of the technology associated with life-saving and fire-fighting are grouped together on the museum's ground floor. The lower ground floor is a real garage which houses a gleaming collection of fire-engines, which have all been restored and are in perfect condition.

On coming out of the museum, turn left in the direction of 'Le Château/Balmont'. After the foundations of La Duchère's old fort on the Boulevard de Balmont have been walked round, the triangular tower of Balmont's former church seems to spring out of the ground. It was built in the 1960s to plans by the architect, Pierre Genton, and has since been converted into both a cinema and a science and work discovery centre called the Musée Interactif Captiva, where children themselves control the machines on display.

New futuristic development in Vaise.

car park, the superb view of the island from the Quai Gillet and the Quai Georges Clemenceau must be seen, as the Romanesque church of Notre-Dame still looks beautiful.

A *prehistoric past*

New light was shed on Lyons' past in 1984 and 1985, during the construction of line D of the metro at Vaise. According to tradition, the city was founded in 43 B.C., but its site has actually been occupied since the Neolithic period (5,000 – 2,500 B.C.), if the excavations carried out in the Gorge-de-Loup area in the far south of Vaise are to be believed. Several hundred years later, it was occupied by Gaulish tribes who traded with the Greeks in the 5th century B.C., as shown by fragments of Greek pottery found in Gorge-de-Loup.

The Romanesque tower of the church of Notre-Dame.

Île Barbe is like an earthen boat surrounded by water.

73

The left bank of the Rhône

CHAPTER 7

The Rhône's former alluvial flood-plain, which suffered from so many floods over the centuries, has finally tamed its river. Up to the 18th century, it was nothing more then a long area of marshland, scattered with islands where cows and sheep grazed. The only human occupation was at La Guillotière, and there principally on its main street which formed part of the highway to the Alps and Italy. The whole of the left bank was brought under its jurisdiction, situated, as it then was, in the Dauphiné region. In 1771, the architect, Jean-Antoine Morand, put forward a development plan for this part of the Rhône valley, and a year later, he built a second bridge to link the two banks, the first bridge, the Pont de la Guillotière, having been built in the Middle Ages. However, a great many disputes with the Hospices Civils de Lyon, which owned part of the land concerned, and then the Revolution and the siege of Lyons delayed the project. The left bank's real urban development had to wait until the reign of Napoleon III, with the laying-out of the quays and river-port on the Rhône, and especially, after the notorious flood of 1856, the construction of an flood-proof embankment, which put an end once and for all to the constant flooding, and, in addition, enabled the safe development of the new district to go ahead.

This visit to the left bank goes from north to south, from the Cité Internationale de Lyon to the new area of Gerland. Further east, the areas of the Etats-Unis, Monplaisir, and Montchat complete this tour, for which, because it covers such a wide area, some form of transport is necessary.

FROM THE CITÉ INTERNATIONALE TO GERLAND

With the Rhône on one side of it and the Parc de la Tête-d'Or on the other, the Cité Internationale stands today on a site between the Quai Charles de Gaulle and the former Quai Achille Lignon, which is now the Allée Achille Lignon. This has rediscovered its original role as a pleasant shady walk alongside the park where nothing but buses pass by. Underground car parks here are a great advantage for car-users.

Construction work was first carried out on the site at the end of the First World War, when the Société de la Foire de Lyon (Lyons Fair Society), with Achille Lignon as its president, decided to build between the park and the river in order to house the annual fair. Edouard Herriot, who had been mayor

Urban development only took place on the left bank of the Rhône from the very end of the 18th century onwards.

75

*The entrance of the Musée
d'Art Contemporain (Museum
of Contemporary Art).*

of Lyons since 1905, gave the green light to the project, and the architect, Charles Meysson, supported by the city's chief engineer, Camille Chalumeau, started work. The 400 metre-long Grand Palais opened its doors in 1928, and many years later, in 1961, it was finished off with the addition of seven exhibition rooms and a Palais des Congrès (conference centre). However, after 50 years on the Quai Achille Lignon, the expansion of the Foire de Lyons forced it to move elsewhere, and in 1984, it went to the eastern suburb of Chassieu and its new, more practical Eurexpo building. The city council and its planning department were well aware of the many assets of the now-vacated site, and so launched a major architectural competition, which was won by Renzo Piano, one of the designers of the Beaubourg in Paris, in order to find a new use for it. Almost all the old buildings were demolished, the only part remaining today being the façade of the former Grand Palais' atrium on the 'park' entrance of the Musée d'Art Contemporain, and gradually, the different elements of the Cité Internationale project got off the ground. Today, the buildings make up a new district in Lyons, focussed on culture, the economy, and leisure. The light and transparent appearance of their architecture is a reflection of that of the greenhouses in the Parc de la Tête-d'Or, terracotta bricks, steel shafts, and large areas of glass being the principal elements of construction. The whole building fits in perfectly with its environment and with the public spaces that have been laid out by the landscape architect, Michel Corajoud, who has worked on the transitional area between the park and the river. A central street following the bend in the Rhône leads to the multiplex cinema on the left, and the Musée d'Art Contemporain on the right, then goes on to the international-class hotel, complete with casino, and then to the Palais des Congrès and the offices of various city businesses. A luxury apartment building is currently nearing completion in the southern part of the site, near Interpol, which was built in 1988, and now finds itself at the gates of the Cité Internationale. Finally, a 3,000-seater lecture theatre, adding the final touch to the Palais des Congrès, will shortly be constructed at the northern end.

The Cité Internationale is a powerful expression of a city which is very firmly orientated towards the future.

The 'Petit Suisse' (Little Switzerland) part of the park with its neatly-cut lawns.

PARC DE LA TÊTE-D'OR

This superb landscaped park covers 105 hectares in a triangle that lies between the Cité Internationale, the Boulevard des Belges, and the Boulevard de Stalingrad in Villeurbanne. Its has been the people of Lyons' favourite place for a walk for 150 years, and on Sundays in spring or summer, the paths wide though they are, are soon crowded, and pushchairs and roller-skaters have a job to push their way through.

It was Claude Marius Vaïsse who took the decision to create the Parc de la Tête-d'Or in February, 1856, as the prefect of the Rhône and mayor of Lyons was worried about the public health of his fellow citizens and wan-

Charles Meysson's monumental wrought-iron gates make a magnificent entrance to the park.

ted to give them a large open-air space where they could relax. To create the park, the city council bought the wooded area of the Tête-d'Or, whose name comes from the fact that a golden head of Christ is supposed to be buried there, and work began immediately, with Denis Bühler, helped by his brother, Eugène, in charge. The architect and landscape architect who several years earlier had contributed to the creation of the Bois de Boulogne in Paris, spent 4 years in designing every element of the park's appearance, which is further embellished by numerous viewpoints of Lyons and its hills. A tour of the park takes hardly an hour, a little more if stops are made to look at the views, and begins at the most imposing entrance, the Porte des Enfants-du-Rhone, at the corner of the Quai Charles de Gaulle and the Boulevard des Belges. The monumental wrought-iron gates by Charles Meyson were only added in 1898, and open on to a lovely view of the 16-hectare lake, which is fed by the waters of the Rhône. The city council took on a large number of Lyons' unemployed to dig the lake, most of whom were silk-workers who were suffering from the loss of their raw material because of a parasitical disease affecting the silk-worms.

'Petite Suisse' (Little Switzerland), which is green and shaded by chestnut trees and conifers, begins on the left, and leads to the Île aux Cygnes (Swan Island) and its war memorial designed by Tony Garnier. Access to the island is through an underground tunnel at the right of the main path, but this is often closed. Afterwards comes the large Roseraie (Rose Garden), which was laid out some what later on in 1964, and whose abundance of 60,000 rose-bushes, made up of 320 different varieties, fills the rose garden with a lovely fragrance in June, when the blooming of the roses is at its peak. A pretty oriental-style bridge then leads to the large island where the cycling track was built in 1894. From the park's belvedere is a lovely view of the lake and the hill of Croix-Rousse. The little train, whose line can be seen on the island, used to be pulled by horses and still takes visitors around the park. Going past the thick woodland and its web of small paths between the Allée du Chalet and the Allée du Grand-Camp, the visitor arrives at the zoo. It was designed by Denis Bühler, and was at first meant to be for farm animals and pets, with fallow deer, (the ancestors of those now to be found in the present 'Parc des Daims'), sheep, and cows being the first tenants. Moreover, it was for them that Tony Garnier built, somewhat later, the now disused municipal cowshed, between 1904 and 1906. In the late 19th century, exotic birds, bears, and crocodiles joined them, and today, almost 750 animals live in buildings that have been specially designed for each species, whether elephants, monkeys, giraffes, or big cats. Behind the zoo, after the Allée du Pré-Fleuri, is the botanical garden, which is the former flower garden of the Place Sathonay at the foot of the slopes of Croix-Rousse, and which was moved to the park during its creation. It groups together several outdoor collections of peonies, aquatic plants, an alpine garden, a garden of old-fashioned roses, and some beautiful 19th century cast-iron and glass greenhouses, which have recently been restored. The small greenhouses, both hot and cold, house orchids, ferns, and flowering plants, whereas the large greenhouses, which have a 21 metre-high central building, are real tropical gardens. Further along on the main path around the park are the Parc aux Daims and the Pelouse de la Coupole (Lawn of the Dome). Some lovely town houses were built along the Allée des

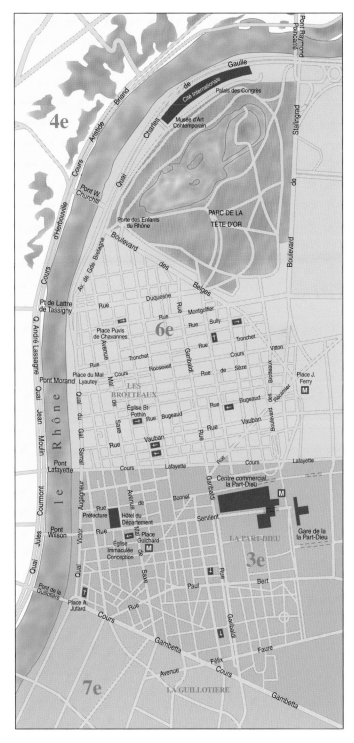

Villas in the late 19th century, and these enjoy superb views of the park. Go round the Pelouse de la Coupole and turn right in the direction of the exit, where some beautiful early 20th century ceramics can be seen on the landing stage.

LES BROTTEAUX

A grand mansion that that has been completely restored on the Boulevard des Belges.

Take the Boulevard des Belges, which runs alongside of the Parc de la Tête-d'Or. This wide boulevard was opened in 1862 on the line of the old fortified walls that were built from 1831 onwards, and the new upper middle-class came to live here in the early 20th century, building private houses along the edge of the park. Gradually, handsome, upper middle-class apartment buildings were constructed on the opposite side of the road, thus confirming the boulevard's 'vocation' as a residential area for the wealthier members of Lyons' population, as well as being the location of several foreign consulates. A short walk beginning at the Boulevard des Brotteaux and finishing at the Pont Lafayette gives a good general idea of the area.

The banks of the Rhône

This pleasant route, which can be followed either on foot or by bicycle, has been laid out over about 9 kilometres (one way only). Starting from the riverbank in the Parc de Gerland, go southwards up to the confluence of the Rhône and Saône, and then northwards, taking in the whole of the left bank, with Gerland, the universities, the Prefecture, Les Brotteaux, and the Cité Internationale, whilst enjoying exceptional views of the Presqu'île. A variation of this walk from the river-port starts around the Pont de Lattre de Tassigny (opposite the Croix-Rousse tunnel) and finishes at the Interpol building. This is the Bretillod educational path, which is equipped with information tables and interactive panels which help the visitor to discover the fauna and flora of the Rhône riverbanks.

Musée d'Histoire Naturelle (Natural History Museum)

This is at number 28, boulevard des Belges, standing back a little from the road. Emile Guinet (1836 – 1918), who came from Lyons, had it built at his own expense in order to house his collection of Far Eastern religious and cultural objects, but he grew weary of the lack of interest shown by the city council, and so moved his museum to Paris in 1888. The unoccupied building then became a 'palais de glace' (ice-skating rink), but that soon ended in failure. Lyons City Council finally bought it in 1911 and restored it to its original role by displaying there Emile Guinet's Egyptian collection. Today, the museum's development is pushing ahead, with its collections now opening up to include different cultures from all over the world.

Continue along the Boulevard des Belges up to the Place Jules Ferry.

Gare des Brotteaux (Les Brotteaux station)

In the centre of the square stands the beautiful façade of the old Les Brotteaux station, which was completed in 1908 to designs by the architect, Paul d'Arbaut. It used to be made up of two parts, a richly decorated passenger building and a steel and glass hall which housed the raised rail tracks, but today only the waiting hall and the façade remain, both protected as listed historical buildings. Several businesses, including one of Paul Bocuse's restaurants, have moved into the building.

Opposite the station, the Brasserie des Brotteaux has preserved its lovely floral mosaics and its old-fashioned counter. At number 1, place Jules Ferry, a block of flats has also kept its Art Nouveau decoration and its stained glass windows in the stairwell.

Take the Rue du Général Brosset, and then the Rue Bugeaud, crossing the Boulevard des Brotteaux, which was constructed in the late 19th century. The church of Saint-Pothin, which can be seen from the Rue Bugeaud, was built in the neo-Classical style by the architect, Crepet, between 1841 and 1843. From the Place Quinet next to the church of Saint-Pothin, is a view of the 1845 Passerelle (footbridge) des Collèges which crosses the Rhône, giving direct access to the Presqu'île and the former Collège de la Trinité, which was taken over by the Jesuits in 1565, and which is today the Lycée Ampère. Take the Avenue de Saxe on the right, admiring its attractive late

The beautiful early 20th century façade of Les Brotteaux' old station.

81

The fountain in the Place Maréchal Lyautey symbolises Lyons and its different characteristic qualities.

19th century apartment buildings, up to the Place du Maréchal Lyautey, where the flower stall was designed by Charles Meysson, who also designed the gate at the main entrance of the Parc de la Tête-d'Or. The impressive fountain of 1865 symbolises Lyons, with its five cherubs representing strength, navigation, commerce, history, and geography. Continue along the Avenue de Saxe and then the Avenue Foch up to the Place Puvis-de-Chavanne on the right, where it took nearly 10 years, from 1868 to 1877, to build the church of the Redemption, with its beautiful stained glass windows. Continue along the Avenue Foch, passing, at number 38, the former governor's house which dates from the mid-19th century. A little further along, at number 28, is the smallest house in Lyons, which is only 2.5 metres wide. The visit ends on the wide roads that border the Rhône, the Quai de Grande Bretagne, the Quai de Serbie, where, at number 11, are statues of Henry IV and Marie de Medici who were married in Lyons on 17th December, 1600, and the Quai du Général Sarrail, where, at number 7, there is a lovely brick house, constructed for the silk merchant, Barioz, in the 1930s, and on which stand two gigantic heads, which can be seen better from the other, Presqu'île, side of the river.

PREFECTURE

The district that runs along the side of the Rhône, from Pont Lafayette to the Pont de la Guillotière, begins at the Quai Victor Augagneur, where the elaborate fronts, at numbers 1, 2, and 4, of the

apartment buildings for Lyons' middle classes bear witness to the late development for housing of this area, which took place from the second half of the 19th century. These buildings stand on either side of the Protestant church, at number 3, that was built by Gaspard André. Continue along the quay to the Pont Wilson (1919), and then take the Rue de Bonnel to the Cours de la Liberté, where the Second Empire architecture of the Prefecture, designed by Louvier in 1890, rises up opposite the Rhône. Four years after it was built, on 24 June, 1894, it was the scene of the death of President Sadi-Carnot, who was quickly moved here from the Rue de la République where the anarchist, Sante Caserio, had just stabbed him as he sat in his carriage. Turn left on the Cours de la Liberté, and stop in front of number 21, in order to admire the Art Nouveau stained glass window behind the gate, then take the Rue de Bonnel, where, at number 9, the apartment building opposite the Prefecture has an inside courtyard and a very beautiful painted ceiling in the entrance hall. Go round the Prefecture by way of the Rue Pierre Corneille to the church of the Immaculate Conception, designed by Pierre Bossan, whose work also includes the church at Fourvière and the church of Saint-Georges, but which was finished by Charles Franchet in 1898. Inside, sturdy pillars give a certain strength to this neo-Romanesque church, which has some beautiful mosaics.

Take the Avenue Maréchal de Saxe on the left behind the church. Here, several entrances to apartment buildings, some of which are unfortunately closed, bear witness to an exceptional wealth of decoration in the late 19th and early 20th century, e.g. the beautiful tiled floor and wide wooden frieze at number 72, the stained glass window at the bottom of the drive at number 76, as well as big bouquets of flowers painted on the walls, which, although they cannot be visited, can be seen from the entrance when the door is open. Almost opposite on the other side of the street, at the corner of the Rue de Bonnel, an old 1930s garage has become a restaurant, but has kept its original distinctive front, which is comparable, on a smaller scale, to that of the Citroën garage that stands on the corner of the Rue de Marseille and the Rue de l'Université (see La Guillotière). Take the Rue de Bonnel and then turn right on the Rue de Vendôme in order to get to the Place Guichard.

Villa Berliet, 39, avenue Esquirol

Marius Berliet (1866 – 1949) was a key figure in the car industry, building up a veritable empire from the late 19th century onwards. In 1910, when his business was booming, this native of Croix-Rousse decided to have a house built in Montchat, where he was already living with his family. Building work, with the architect, Paul Bruyas, in charge, began in 1911, while the interior decoration was assigned to two renowned artists, Louis Majorelle and Jacques Gruber. The stucco friezes, mosaic floors, windows painted with floral patterns, and mahogany furniture are today the finest example of Art Nouveau in Lyons. Since 1982, the villa has housed the Fondation Berliet, whose function is to safeguard and promote the region's automobile heritage. It is open to the public during the weekend of the 'Journées de la Patrimoine' (Heritage Days) every September.

BOURSE DU TRAVAIL (TRADES UNION CENTRE)

In 1930, the mayor of Lyons, Edouard Herriot, entrusted the construction of the Bourse de Travail to his chief archi-

tect, Charles Meysson (the designer of the gates at the Parc de la Tête-d'Or), helped by his colleague, Baud. The frontage is plain and geometric, but does have some decoration in the form of a

The Bourse du Travail: a building designed by Lyons' chief architect, Charles Meysson, with a mural by Ferdinand Fargeot.

large mosaic by Ferdinand Fargeot, which depicts Edouard Herriot and part of his city council. The interior has been refurbished so that concerts and shows can be held there, but the atrium has not been touched. From the Place Guichard, take the Rue de Créqui, then the Rue Servient, and finally, the Rue Moncey, which comes out at the back of the Halles (Indoor Market). This temple of gastronomy was built in the early 1970s, and is packed with mainly regional specialities. People come to the warm and welcoming atmosphere here to have a snack of a dozen oysters, or to buy a good Saint-Marcellin cheese, or a sau-

Concerts are not only organised inside the Auditorium, but also in the area just outside it.

sage to cook. On the Cours Lafayette, outside the Halles, are two long blocks of flats whose architectural style is that of Corbusier, and which were designed by one of his pupils, Zumbrunnen.

LA PART-DIEU

The present-day business centre in Lyons replaced a disused 19th century military barracks, which was purchased by Lyons City Council in 1960 before eventually being demolished to make way for the construction of a shopping centre, the Crédit Lyonnais tower, and the Auditorium Maurice Ravel. Other administrative buildings and offices joined them to form what is today a coherent unit of contemporary architecture. It does not take long to visit the area, starting from the Part-Dieu shopping centre (Part-Dieu metro station, and tramway and bus stop), and only requires a few stops at the main places of interest.

LA PART-DIEU
SHOPPING CENTRE

When it was opened in September, 1975, it was Europe's largest shopping centre, covering 220,000 square metres, of which 110,000 square metres is made up of retail premises, and was designed by the architects, Charles Delfente and Régis Seller. It has 260 shops spread over three galleries, and is visited by up to 100,000 people every day. It is currently being refurbished. At the Porte de l'Esplanade on level 2, there is access to the Auditorium Maurice Ravel and the Crédit Lyonnais tower. The **Auditorium Maurice Ravel,** designed by the architects Delfante, Pottier, Caille, and Reichsteiner, was opened in 1975, and has a surprising effect because of its curious design in the form of a shell, closed in on itself, which is clearly visible from the steps of the Place Général de Gaulle, the square in front of the Auditorium. Inside, the absence of pillars adds to the lightness of the space. This enormous hall has more than 2,000 seats, and is the venue for concerts by the Orchestre National de Lyon as well as other international orchestras.

The Crédit Lyonnais tower, designed by the architect, Araldo Cossuta, was completed in 1977. Its pointed dome looks like the tip of a pencil, hence its nickname of the 'Crayon' (Pencil), and rises up to 165 metres in height above the Rue Servient. It has 30 floors of

La Part-Dieu station with the Ipousteguy fountain in the foreground.

Lyons' famous 'Crayon' (pencil), whose point dominates the area of La Part-Dieu.

offices and 10 floors given over to a 4-star hotel. The panoramic view of Lyons from the restaurant is absolutely superb.

Go back to the shopping centre, and take the Porte de la Bibliothèque (level 2) to enter the concrete **Bibliothèque Centrale de Lyon** (Central Library), which has a stock of 2 million books. Leave by the Porte Vivier-Merle on level 1 in the direction of the Gare de La Part-Dieu, which is separated from the shopping centre by the Boulevard Vivier-Merle. The Place Charles Béraudier, with its monumental clock and a fountain designed by Ipousteguy in 1987, lies opposite. The square is in front of the station, which was designed by the architects, Gachon and Girodet, and opened in 1993, and whose great distinctive feature is its hall, which lies beneath railway tracks 120 metres long.

Finally, make your way towards the La Guillotière district by following the Boulevard Vivier-Merle up to the Rue Paul Bert. This is a very lively area that has been the home of a North African community since the 1930s.

LA GUILLOTIÈRE

The district commonly called 'La Guill' runs from the Pont de la Guillotière to the Pont Gallieni, and goes back as far as the Boulevard de Tchécoslovaquie, which marks the beginning of Monplaisir. La Guillotière became part of Lyons in 1852 at the same time as Vaise and Croix-Rousse, and today is home to a mixture of all sorts of people, such as craftsmen, small shopkeepers, students, and immigrants from Italy, North Africa, and Asia. It is a real pleasure to go for a walk through the area, taking the time to push open doors and to talk to the people who live here.

Logically enough, the tour begins at the Pont de la Guillotière, which in the 12th century was the old wooden bridge, in fact the only bridge, that linked the Lyonnais region with that of Dauphiné. Its importance is such that the people of Lyons still call the Place Gabriel Péri, the 'Place du Pont'. To get there, first of all walk through the 'Fosse aux Ours' (Bear Pit), an underground passage whose circular part is open to the sky, then the Place Jutard where the early 20th century Palais de la Mutualité is to be found, and finally, a small part of the Cours Gambetta. The Place Gabriel Péri is an important crossroads for bus, metro, and tram, and is still an extremely popular meeting place for the people of Lyons. This is the starting point for the historic highway of the Grande Rue de la Guillotière, which has led to the Alps and, still further on, to Italy since the Middle Ages. The old Hostel des Trois Rois, at the corner of the street with the same name, bears witness to this period with a wall-plaque displaying the dates of 1190 – 1834. It was restored in the 19th century, and is today divided up into flats, with a shop on the ground floor. A very attractive wrought iron balcony opposite

85

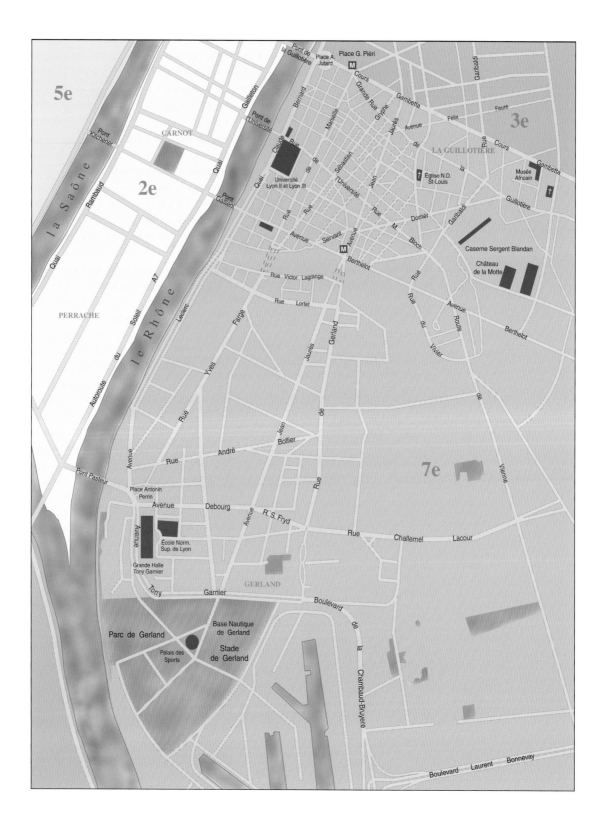

overlooks the Rue des Trois Rois.

Follow the Cours Gambetta up to the Boulevard de Tchécoslovaquie, where, at number 33, a new block of flats has replaced the old Eldorado theatre, which was demolished without much forethought. Some attractive apartment buildings are worth stopping to take a brief look at, e.g. middle-class house fronts at number 47 and on the Place Victor Basch, the Maison du Cheval Blanc at number 76, a large blue carriage entrance at number 78, and a beautiful building with an enclosed balcony at number 87. At number 150, the Musée des Missions Africaines displays a great number of objects, such as masks, jewels, and weights and measures, that have come from West Africa. On the right at the end of the Cours Gambetta, on the other side of the Boulevard de Tchécoslovaquie, stands the old Manufacture des Tabacs (Cigarette Factory), which dates from the early 20th century, and which has been completely refurbished to form part of the University of Lyons 3 – Jean Moulin. Follow the Boulevard de Tchécoslovaquie up to the Grande Rue de la Guillotière, and then turn right. Former coaching inns, craftsmen's workshops, sheds, and new blocks of flats line this street which has retained its winding, medieval path. Worth a

look are number 134, a very old, dilapidated house which is very probably doomed to be demolished, but which has an interior courtyard and a mosaic frieze on its pediment, as well as number 131, which has arches and gilded stones. The former Hôtel de l'Aigle, standing between numbers 109 and 105, bears an inscription stating that Napoleon passed by here on his return to France from the island of Elba. Just opposite, at number 102, which was undoubtedly an old coa-

A handsome building: the former Manufacture des Tabacs has been completely restored and is now a university hall of residence.

The University Claude Bernard Lyons 3 stands, beautifully floodlit, on the banks of the Rhône.

The Resistance in Lyons

The armistice that France signed with Germany in 1940 forced it to divide its territory into two. Lyons was situated in the free zone until 1942, and became a major centre of resistance, with newspapers and resistance groups being formed, supported by several clandestine printing presses. At the end of 1941, Jean Moulin, a symbolic Resistance figure, came to Lyons in order to unite the three southern networks of Combat, Franc-Tireur, and Libération, which became the 'Mouvement Uni de la Résistance' (United Resistance Movement) in 1942. Six months later, on 21 June, 1943, he was arrested at Caluire and transferred to Montluc prison before suffering interrogation at the hands of Klaus Barbie, and dying before being transported to Germany. A mural by the Cité de la Création on one of the Montluc prison walls (Rue du Dauphiné) pays tribute to the former Resistance fighter.

ching inn, a carriage entrance leads to a lovely cobbled courtyard, which is unfortunately in a bad state of repair. Go back up the main street, passing close to the Caserne (Barracks) du Sergent Blandan, which conceals one of Lyons' historical treasures, the Château de la Motte, an old 16th century estate situated at the gates of Lyons, whose guests included kings and queens of France and senior Church dignitaries. After the Revolution, the château became part of the Fort de Lamothe, which later became the Caserne du Sergent Blandan. The château was listed as an historical monument on the Inventaire Complémentaire des Monuments Historiques in 1983, but is unfortunately not open to the public. However, its external architecture, that of a square formed by its buildings with square and round towers, is clearly visible from the Rue du Repos, which runs alongside the barracks in the direction of the Rue de l'Epargne, and then the Rue Marius Berliet. Continue along the Grande Rue de la Guillotière to the corner of the Rue de la Madeleine. The neo-Classical church of Saint-Louis was built in the 19th century by the architect, Christophe Crépet. Inside the entrance, on the Rue de la Madeleine side, is a painting by the Lyons artist, Jean Scohy (1824 – 1897) depicting the floods of 1856, which wreaked havoc in this part of La Guillotière. Opposite is an extremely beautiful 11th century stoup (the first on the left) and stained glass windows by Louis Guy. The Rue de la Madeleine, which leads to the Place Saint-Louis, is very attractive, with the old carriage entrance at the sign of the 'Lampisterie' at number 16 and, more especially, the arched passage in the Rue Saint-Michel, opposite the Fire Station, adding to its charm. After the Place Saint-Louis, take the Rue Saint-Lazare to the Rue Marcel Bloch, and then the Rue de l'Université. The eyes are then drawn towards the impressive Citroën Building, constructed in reinforced concrete by Jacques Ravazé between 1930 and 1932, which stands at the corner of the Rue de Marseille. This is four-sided in shape, but only two of the sides are parallel, and it has two corner towers. The university area is then entered, with, to right and left of the Rue de l'Université, facing the Rhône, two imposing late 19th century buildings by the same architect, Abraham Hirsch. To the left at number 15, quai Claude Bernard, where the arts faculty used to be sited, is the law faculty of the University of Lyons 3 – Claude Bernard. Further on is the Rhône swimming pool, which is easily identifiable

A path in the Parc Gerland.

because of its pylons which rise up above the Rhône. To the right, between numbers 16 and 18, the former faculty of medicine now forms part of the University of Lyons 2 – Lumière, and between these two university buildings, the road leads to the beautiful Pont de l'Université, which crosses over to the Presqu'île. A visit after dark is essential for the classical beauty of these different buildings to be really appreciated, as it is then that the quays by the side of the Rhône are illuminated with a bluish-white light, a daily spectacle of which the people of Lyons never tire. Leave La Guillotière after visiting the Musée de la Résistance et de la Déportation at 14, avenue Berthelot, which leads off the end of the Quai Claude Bernard), where the poignant audiovisual and photographic accounts have an even stronger effect because they are displayed in a building used by the Gestapo during the Second World War.

GERLAND

This huge area was for a long time the site of heavy industries, with, for example, chemical works, metal industries, the Edouard Herriot port, and abattoirs, but its appearance is now gradually changing. It has been christened the 'Nouvelle Rive Gauche' (New Left Bank), and is today a scientific, university, and high technology centre. The focus for any pleasant visit to the area will be on the paths through the Parc Gerland, which gives a good overview of the early 20th century buildings, mainly those built by Tony Garnier, as well as those more modern in date. The visit begins in the Place Antonin Perrin, in front of the Halle Tony Garnier (Parking near-by).

THE GRANDE HALLE (GREAT HALL) OR HALLE TONY GARNIER

This old cattle market is today the symbol of Gerland. When it was completed in 1914, it formed an integral part of the plan for the construction of the De La Mouche abattoirs, designed by Tony Garnier. It was one of the pavilions in the 1914 International Exhibition, was then used as a munitions factory during the First World War, and did not actually become a cattle market until 1928. Today, it is the only remaining evidence of the old abattoirs which occupied a site of 25 hectares, and whose activity has now been transferred to Corbas, out in the suburbs of Lyons. The hall became a listed historical monument in 1975, and has been completely renovated to enable concerts and exhibitions to be held there. Its 120 metre-high metallic framework is quite a feat, as this beautiful

Lightness and movement in architecture: the Lycée International.

example of industrial architecture seems to have no form of support. Behind the hall on the left-hand side is the ENS (Ecole Normale Supérieure Sciences – a 'grande école' or kind of specialist university), which has occupied the site of the old abattoirs since 1987. However, nothing remains of these abattoirs but a single arch which serves as the pedestrian entrance to the hall side of the ENS Sciences, and is thus a symbol of the historic passage between the two buildings.

Take the Avenue Tony Garnier which runs alongside the hall on its right-hand side, past the headquarters building of Pasteur-Mérieux Connaught, the Agence

The Halle Tony Garnier with its stunning metal framework is Gerland's outstanding landmark.

89

The Ecole Nationale Supérieure des Sciences stands behind the former abattoirs.

de l'Eau, and finally, the Lycée International, a beautiful glass building designed by the architects, Françoise Jourda and Gilles Perraudin. This marks the beginning of the Parc de Gerland, a very large, flat playground bordered by the Rhône and the Avenue Tony Garnier and Avenue Jean Bouin. It will eventually cover an area of 80 hectares, and encompass the Palais de Sports and Stade de Gerland. Along the banks of the Rhône, a 'fog system', which diffuses an extremely fine mist that creates mini rainbows when the sun shines, has been installed. Make your way along the park's central walk, which is fringed with rectangular ponds where aquatic plants grow, to enjoy lovely views of the different buildings in the area, e.g. the Aguettant laboratories and then the Skate Park, where roller-skating and skateboarding fans come to practise. Further on, the eye-catching egg-shaped dome that is 90 metres in diameter forms part of the Palais de Sports. Turn left at the corner of the Skate Park, past some small allotment gardens, and go to one of the park entrances, where, on the left, a mural depicts the main events of the 1998 World Cup. Turn right up the Avenue Pierre de Coubertin up to the Stade de Gerland. This was built from 1913 onwards by Tony Garnier in the spirit of the stadiums of Ancient Rome as its four entrances are triumphal arches. It was meant to form part of a vast sporting complex, a project that was later abandoned, but its capacity was increased to 43,000 covered places for the 1998 World Cup. After a tour of the stadium, turn

The Ecole Nationale Supérieure des Lettres building was designed by the architects, Henri and Bruno Gaudin.

90

left back onto on the Avenue Tony Garnier, and return to the Halle Tony Garnier following the pedestrian path that runs alongside it.

To see Gerland in greater depth, take a short trip round the area by car. From the Place Antonin Perrin, take the Avenue Debourg, leaving behind on your left the new Ecole Nationale Supérieure Lettres et Sciences Humaines (Arts and Social Sciences), that was designed by the architects, Henri Gaudin (the school) and his son, Bruno Gaudin (the library, which is open to the public). Afterwards, turn right onto the Avenue Jean Jaurès, then left onto the Rue Challemel-Lacour. It was around this street that a garden-suburb was built during the 1930s, with pinkish 4-storey blocks of flats with lattice-work balconies. Return by the Rue Simon Fryd, and then the Avenue de Debourg up to the Place Antonin Perrin.

FROM ETATS-UNIS TO MONTCHAT

To the east of Gerland, a belt of urban development joins up three districts that lie one next to the other, Etat-Unis, Monplaisir, and Montchat. This last route begins on the left bank on the Boulevard des Etats-Unis, between the Rue Paul Cazenave and Rue Jean Sarrazin (numbers 62 to 86 of the Boulevard des Etats-Unis). Some means of transport, mainly the metro, even though it does not go to Etats-Unis, or a car are essential if the trip is to be done in one go.

CITÉ TONY GARNIER

On both sides of the Boulevard des Etats-Unis stretches the chequer-board housing development conceived by the Lyons architect, Tony Garnier, and completed in 1934. It was planned to house about 12,000 people, and was built around a principal thoroughfare, the Boulevard des Etats-Unis, and several secondary roads. Small two- or three-storey blocks of flats are separated from each other by landscaped areas, thus forming a very pleasant environment in which to live. Although Tony Garnier's initial plan has undergone some modifications, such as the reduction in size of the plots of land and gardens, together with the heightening of the flats to 5 storeys, this development, which was restored during the 1980s, is nevertheless a brilliant architectural success. It

Tony Garnier (1869–1948)

Tony Garnier was born in Lyons of a father who was a designer in the silk trade and a mother who was a weaver. He first studied drawing at Lyons' Ecole des Beaux-Arts (art school) before going to Paris. In 1889, he was awarded the Grand Prix de Rome, and worked on his project of an industrial development, which was in fact a condensed version of the buildings that he was to build later. The municipal dairy of 1905 in the Parc de la Tête-d'Or was his first construction in his home town. After meeting Edouard Herriot, he became Lyons' major projects architect and has left his mark on several sites, including the De La Mouche abattoirs, whose great hall, a well-known example of industrial architecture, is still standing, the Gerland football stadium, the war memorial on the Île des Cygnes in the Parc de la Tête-d'Or, the Edouard Herriot hospital, and the Etats-Unis housing estate. His last work was not in Lyons as it was the town hall in Boulogne-Billancourt in the Paris region.

One of the 24 murals that are painted on side-walls in the Cité de la Création.

is a very attractive, delightful place to visit, with its bow-windows and its pedestrian paths ornamented with pergolas. Walk from one street to another to admire the 24 murals painted on the buildings' side walls, of which 16 depict the architect's major projects, 6 are the work of international artists, and 2 act as information panels. Begin the walk at number 1, rue des Serpollières, in front of three two- and three-storey buildings that were built in 1924, and which were the prototypes of Tony Garnier's initial plan. At number 4, the branch museum of the Musée Urbain Tony Garnier has a

Auguste and Louis Lumière, the inventors of the first cinematograph in 1895.

Today, the Lumière brothers' château keeps the memory of the cinematograph alive.

collection of plans and photographs of the site, and is also the meeting place for a guided tour of the museum and of the show flat, which has been fitted out and furnished by the local tenants. This 3-roomed flat at number 8, rue des Serpollières looks as though it has always lived in, and shows the estate's been original domestic decor, with its typical 1930s furniture and decoration.

If travelling by car, follow the Boulevard des Etats-Unis up to the Boulevard Laurent Bonnevay, turn left onto it, then come off it on to the Boulevard Pinel. If travelling by bus, tram, or metro, get off at the 'Laennec' stop. Lyons' Grande Mosquée (Great Mosque) stands at 146, boulevard Pinel, and this beautiful white building, constructed in 1994, can be visited every day except Friday.

INSTITUT LUMIÈRE

Go to the Place Ambroise Courtois in Monplaisir. If travelling by car, take the Avenue Laennec from the Boulevard Pinel, and then the Cours Albert Thomas, which leads there, and if using the bus, tram, or metro, get off at the 'Montplaisir-Lumière' stop.

A circular monument in the square commemorates the Lumière brothers, who invented the first cinematograph in 1895. Auguste and Louis Lumière lived and worked for over 50 years at the Château Lumière, a lovely upper middle-class house that their father, Antoine, built right at the beginning of the 20th century on the Place Ambroise Courtois. Seen from the park, whose entrance is at 25, rue du Premier-Film, it has retained its distinguished appearance with its superb winter garden, decorated with stained glass. At the bottom of the park used to stand the Lumière brothers' factory where they made their first film, 'Sortie des Usines Lumières' (Leaving the Lumières' Factory), and of which only the hangar remains, miraculously saved from demolition, and now forming part of a complex comprising a new cinema screen, which specialises in the showing of 'art house' and experimental films. The Château Lumière is today the headquarters of the Institut Lumière, which aims to promote the cinema in general and the work of the Lumière brothers in particular.

EDOUARD HERRIOT HOSPITAL

From the Place Ambroise Courtois, take the Cours Albert Thomas, either on foot, or, if using the metro, get off at the Grange-Blanche stop, to the Place de l'Arsonval. Shöffer's 1992 luminous totem pole, which is multicoloured come nightfall, stands opposite the Hôpital Edouard Herriot's main entrance. The hospital was designed by Tony Garnier to be a low-rise multi-wing building, and was opened by the mayor of Lyons, Edouard Herriot, in 1933. In it can be found the Lyons architect's characteristic design features, such as recessed walls, gardens, and pergolas, which give a more human face to this hospital complex, all parts of which are linked by a very clever network of underground corridors to avoid the patients having to go outside.

Edouard Herriot (1872–1957)

To say that Edouard Herriot really left his mark on the city is only too obvious, as he was Lyons' mayor for over 50 years, from 1905 to 1957, with just one interruption, from 1942 to 1945, during the Second World War. This very highly educated man became a member of the Radical Party at the time of the Dreyfus Affair. Parallel to his 'reign' in Lyons, he had an extremely busy political and social life, being senator and deputy for the Rhône, a minister several times, president of the Council, president of the Chamber of Deputies and of the National Assembly, and a member of the Académie Française. To him Lyons owes some of its major facilities, which were mainly constructed by Tony Garnier, as well as several pieces of writing, including 'Lyon n'est plus' (Lyons no longer exists), in reference to the siege of Lyons during 1793 and 1794.

The allotments alongside the Parc Chambouvet are a tradition that endures to this day.

MONTCHAT

Cross the whole length of the hospital to reach the peaceful district of Montchat. Turn right onto the Rue Viala. After the Place Claudia, turn right onto the Rue de Trarieux which rises gently, and where pretty houses with gardens stand on both sides of the street. These were built in the 19th century for people on small incomes on plots of land of less than 1,000 square metres, which were given by the Richard-Vittons, an important property owning family in Montchat. Furthermore, the family's Christian names have been used to name several streets, e.g. Julie, Julien, Antoinette, and Camille. To the left, take the Impasse Pommier which opens into the Parc Chambouvet. This stands on a small hill with panoramic views of Lyons, and has small allotments around its edge. There is a very pleasant way down from the park towards the centre of Montchat by way of the Place Charles Dufraine, then the Rue Pierre Bonot, and the Rue Constant (to the right) which leads to the Place du Château. The church of Notre-Dame-de-Bon-Secours, which was built in 1883, and the château, which underwent alterations in the 19th century, and which has since been converted into a conference centre, are attractive features of this small village square. Behind the square runs Montchat's main thoroughfare, the busy shopping street of the Rue Docteur Long, which leads to the Place Henri, from where it is possible to follow the Avenue Lacassagne, which is not very interesting at all except for its two murals created by the Cité de la Création. There is a mural depicting Lyons' great scientists and doctors at number 115, and another illustrating a history of public transport in Lyons at number 98. Just before number 34 is a beautiful, large building dating from 1900, whose sculptures of bunches of grapes are a reminder of its first use, which is still engraved on its pediment, the 'Grandes Caves de Lyon' (Great Wine Cellars of Lyons). It has been converted into a house, and will soon be integrated into a new flat-building project.

93

Villeurbanne

CHAPTER 8

This sizeable city of more than 100,000 inhabitants is bordered and then crossed by the Boulevard Laurent Bonnevay ring road, and likes to think of itself as Lyons' rival. Its coat of arms depicts a dolphin ('dauphin' in French, representing Villeurbanne's former region of the Dauphiné) facing the lion of Lyons, and it has been successful in asserting its own personality, which has always been very modern in attitude.

The origins of Villeurbanne go a long way back in time to a place called Les Tasses, which lay between the present-day square and cemetery in Cusset, and which was not, in principle, a very satisfactory site as it was marshland. However, the village managed to keep going, due to the fact that the Rhône's alluvial soils were very fertile, but its real growth did not take place until the mid-19th century, after the area's drainage due to the cutting through of the Canal de Jonage and the construction of dykes. Lyons was beginning to become cramped for space, and so many of its industrial companies established themselves on Villeurbanne's flat open spaces, and so from being just a village, it became an industrial and commercial city, lying between the two areas of Cusset and Les Charpennes. The first phase of urban development created the Tonkin estate, which is a collection of small late-19th century working-class houses. The

*The Villeurbanne
skyscrapers.*

Opposite:
*The Maison du Livre, de l'Image, et du Son
(Book, Image, and Sound Centre) was
designed by the architect, Mario Botta.*

second, and much more important, phase came about in 1930 when the mayor, Lazare Goujon (1869–1960) proposed a complete rethink of the city. As the Compagnie d'Applications Mécaniques had sold its land in 1925, this Socialist doctor who wanted 'to change the town in order to change people's lives' launched one of the first great town planning operations in France. He wanted to create a new area for the working-classes where there would be low-cost, comfortable housing with running water, gas, electricity, bathrooms and toilets, central heating, and mechanical household waste disposal units. He also wanted to create a new city centre with a town hall and a Palais du Travail, which would be a centre for cultural, sporting, and trades union activities. The resulting Gratte-Ciel (Sky-scraper) area was constructed by Môrice Leroux and Robert Giroud.

During the post-war years, and always under the leadership of Socialist mayors (Gagnaire, Hernu, and Chabron after Goujon, who was re-elected in 1947 and 1953), the city continued its progress in the field of culture. In 1957, a scientific university campus opened at La Doua, near Tonkin, on the old race course, and Roger Planchon, the actor and director, took charge of the Théâtre de la Cité near the Palais du Travail. In 1982, a new museum of contemporary art opened its doors at 11, rue du Docteur Dolard, and in 1988, the Maison du Livre, de l'Image, et du Son (Book, Image, and Sound Museum) was completed. The old parts of Villeurbanne have been renovated or even completely replanned as part of the town planning process.

The following three walks give a good idea of the city's modernity and progress.

CUSSET

Thanks to the metro ('Cusset' station, in the direction of Laurent Bonnevay), it is possible to go back to Villeurbanne's origins, to the village which the city once was. There are few remains of this early modern period, just the former church of Saint-Julien-des-Mariniers, which is now the Ukrainian Orthodox church of Sainte-Athanase, and a few streets around the curving Rue Eugène Réguillon Baratin which goes round the village. What is remarkable in Cusset is the large number of stadiums (Lyvet, Bopiron, Granger, Iris, and Séverine) and sporting facilities that are concentrated in the area. Visit the Jardin des Mille Couleurs (Garden of a Thousand Colours), which is a reminder of the diversity of the people who have come to live in Villeurbanne, a diversity which has helped it to grow.

Two 19-storey towers form the entrance to the Gratte-Ciel (Skyscraper) district.

97

GRATTE-CIEL

The Maison du Livre, de l'Image, et du Son's interior revolves around a cone of light.

Take the metro to 'Gratte-Ciel' station, in the direction of Perrache. Coming out of the station, the visitor first thinks that he must be somewhere else, and then feels that he is in a kind of time warp, as the two 19-storey towers opposite form the entrance to a 4.5 hectare district, and on each side of the 18-metre wide Avenue Henri Barbusse stand six identical 9- to 11-storey white blocks. An expert eye can recognise the influence of the stepped buildings in the garden-suburbs designed by the Parisian, Henri Sauvage (1873–1932), the recessed walls of Eugène Hénard's buildings, and the Art Deco designs of the inter-war period. You have to be either an architect or to have worked on the restoration of the buildings between 1992 and 1998 to know that these 1,500 flats have a metal framework and brick walls.

Blocking the view at the top of the avenue is the town hall, which makes a complete break in style with the blocks of

flats. The massive neo-Classical style used by Giroud and the monumental belfry give the building a very solid look. Inside, however, the decoration is Art Deco.

Behind the town hall on the Place Lazare Goujon, the former Palais du Travail, a plainer building by Môrice Leroux, houses the Théâtre National Populaire (TNP), a swimming pool, and some premises used for social and cultural activities. On the square itself, ponds, pergolas, plant holders decorated with inter-war bas-reliefs, and more recent statues – 'La République Enchaînée' (The Republic in Chains) by Georges Salendre (1946) and the bust of Lazare Goujon by Jean-Louis Chorel (1967) – help to make the visitor feel as though he is in another age. The whole of the square is, quite naturally, classed as a 'zone de protection du patrimoine architectural, urbain, et paysager' (protected architectural, urban, and landscape area).

On the way back to the metro station, the Maison du Livre, de l'Image, et du Son, comprising 3,500 square metres of library, record and video libraries, an auditorium, and an art library, can be visited at 247, cours Emile Zola. It is the work of Mario Botta, and formed part of the important state-promoted architectural projects undertaken in France in the 1980s. The building has a flat black and white façade, and is constructed from stone, concrete, metal, and glass. The central glass screen reveals the Maison's internal structure of six levels around which run landings, while inside, everything is arranged around a cone of light.

FROM LES CHARPENNES TO LA DOUA

The whole of this area has been restructured since the late 1960s, and contains buildings characteristic of the different architectural and planning trends over the last 30 years. Gérard Gasquet's giant mural has grabbed people's attention at the exit of Les Charpennes station, at 20 and 22, cours Emile Zola, ever since 1982. Take the Rue Descartes to the Avenue Roger Salengro, which follows on from the Avenue Galline, in order to get to Tonkin, where several streets (Son-Tay, Hanoi, and Bat-Yam) still have names which recall France's colonisation of the former Indo-China, which was at its peak at the time that this housing development was created. However, the working-class atmosphere of this district, where a flea-market used to be held every Sunday morning, is very hard to find. Office buildings, of which the most prestigious are in the Boulevard Stalingrad, on the edge of the Parc de la Tête-d'Or, and near La Part-

Dieu station, and blocks of flats have sprung up all over, sometimes breaking up the old highway network, as is shown by the fact that the Rue Son-Tay has been cut in two. The Cité des Antiquaires (Antiques Centre) is open to visitors in the Central Park building, constructed by the AAMCO agency in 1989 and 1990. The Sunday morning flea-market has, however, been forced to move away to the Avenue Monin and Rue de la Feyssine at the other side of the ring-road.

Carry on northwards, to where the La Doua campus has stood along the Boulevard du 11 Novembre since 1958. Sited on the campus today are the Université Claude Bernard, the Institut National des Sciences Appliquées (National Institute of Applied Sciences), the Ecole Nationale des Sciences de l'Information et des Bibliothèques (Information Science and Library School), the Ecole Supérieure de Chimie (a 'grande école' specialising in chemistry), INSERM (Institut National de la Santé et de la Recherche Médicale – National Institute for Medical Research), and the regional centre of the CNRS (Centre National de la Recherche Scientifique – National Centre for Scientific Research, similar to the UK's Science Research Council).

The Théâtre National Populaire (TNP)

The Théâtre National Populaire was relocated from the Palais de Chaillot in Paris, where Roger Planchon had been director of the Théâtre de la Cité since 1958, to Villeurbanne in 1972 as part of a decentralisation project. In the tradition of Jean Dasté and after having directed at the small Marroniers Theatre, Roger Planchon put on classic plays, which showed his predilection for Brecht, Shakespeare, and Molière. Season tickets and agreements negotiated with works councils and educational establishments enabled new audiences to go to the theatre, and so never was gratitude to a person better deserved. Subsequently, however, the TNP's development has been due to substantial financial resources, institutionalisation, and social and cultural changes.

Suggested routes in the Lyons area

CHAPTER 9

Beautiful as the city may be, sometimes you feel the need to get out of it to enjoy the wider horizons of the countryside. One of Lyons' distinctive features is that leaving town in any direction is very quick and easy, as it takes less than 30 minutes to leave the city behind. There are so many possible routes, but three itineraries are suggested here – westwards, to the Monts du Lyonnais, northwards, to the Saône Valley and Monts d'Or, and, beyond that, to the Beaujolais.

MONTS DU LYONNAIS

This is a favourite trip for the people of Lyons, as many of them have second homes in the country on the final slopes of the Massif Central. Once past Vaise, two possibilities present themselves.

Following the N 6, go to Charbonnières-les-Bains, which has been famous since the 18th century for its thermal springs, and, since 1894, for its, now renovated, casino, known since 1987 as the Rhône Vert. The village, like all those

Charbonnières-les-Bains' casino was built in 1894, and renovated in 1987.

Opposite:
The village of Theizé.

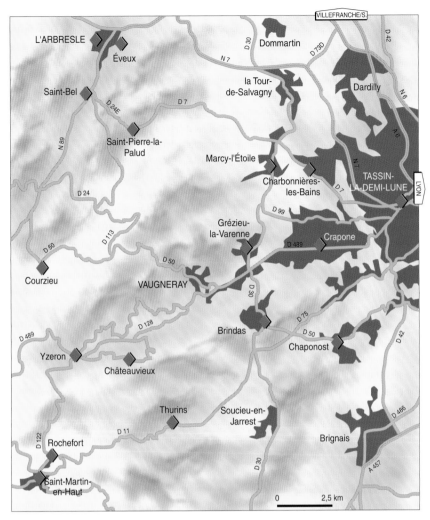

in the west Lyonnais area, is a rather posh residential area, lying in the middle of the original trees that were planted here in the 19th century. Take the D 30 to Marcy-l'Etoile and the Lacroix-Laval estate, a former property of the counts of Lacroix-Laval, which has been open to the public since 1985. Its many visitors find here an elegant old château, renovated by Soufflot in the 18th century,

The château of Lacroix-Laval near Marcy-l'Etoile was restored by Soufflot in the 18th century.

A doll museum unique in France is housed in the château of Lacroix-Laval.

and over-restored in the early 20th century and again in 1990, which houses a doll museum that is unique in France. A large formal flowerbed and a lake stretch out in front of the château, but it is the natural environment which is the real attraction here. Renovation work has preserved the spirit of the landscaped park, which opens out onto meadows, clearings, ponds, forests, greenhouses, a farm, a vegetable garden, and a deer park, all of which can be explored thanks to 14 kilometres of paths. Nearby are the Institut National de Travail (National Institute of work), the Ecole Vétérinaire (School of Veterinary Medicine), which was founded in Lyons in 1761 and moved here in 1977, and Mérieux, a company specialising in vaccine manufacture, which has been here since 1917. Continue on the D 7 to Saint-Pierre-la-Palud, a mining town where iron pyrites essential for the making of sulphuric acid were extracted until 1972, as shown by the pit head frame, the miners' houses, and a museum. In the 19th century, a branch of the Mangini family, who are famous in the region for having been responsible for the construction of the Lyons – Montbrison railway, had the Château de la Perollière built here by Gaspard André, in the style of a Floren-

Entrance doorway at the château of La Pérollière at Saint-Pierre-la-Palud.

103

Reconstruction of life down the mine at Saint-Pierre-la-Palud.

The Saint-Pierre-la-Palud mining museum.

104

tine villa. Further along the D 7 lies Sain-Bel, which owes its name to the fact that Charles VIII found it to be 'saine et belle' (healthy and beautiful). The town is overlooked by the old Château de Montbloy (12th, 15th, and 19th centuries) which was originally built to protect the 10th century Savigny Abbey, less than

Saint-Pierre-la-Palud's mine produced the iron pyrites needed for the manufacture of sulphuric acid until 1972.

L'Arbresle was the birthplace of the inventor of the sewing-machine.

The château of La Péollière was built in the late 19th century by Gaspard André in the style of Florentine villas.

3 kilometres away. Today, all that is left is the 12th century keep (known as the 'Tour de l'Horloge' or clock tower), some Renaissance style houses, stones that have been reused in the walls of various houses or collected together for display in a small museum, and a lovely 13th century Virgin inside the church. The N 496 can be taken to return to Lyons, passing through l'Arbresle, the birthplace of Barthélémy Thimonnier, the inventor of the sewing machine, whose life, together with the industrial history of the weaving town, is recalled in the Musée du Vieil Arbresle. The 15th century church has a neo-Gothic clock tower and early 16th century stained glass windows. In the neighbouring village of Eveux, religious art can also be seen in the monastery of Sainte-Marie-de-la-Tourette, which was constructed in shuttered concrete between 1956 and 1959 to plans by Le Corbusier. The Dominican community that lives there opens its doors every Sunday morning for Mass, and also for research seminars, or for individual stays. The almost windowless church, cloister, chapter house,

*The monastery
of Sainte-Marie-de-la-Tourette
in the village of Eveux.*

In designing the monastery, Le Corbusier gave it very pure lines and exquisite colours.

lecture rooms, library, about 100 monks' cells, and, in the park, an 18th century ice house can then all be seen. From here, return to the N 7.

Alternatively, go through Tassin-la-Demi-Lune to Craponne, and then take the D 489 to where Yzeron stands perched on its rock. Until the 1960s, the village was the people of Lyons' favourite holiday spot, but today its is no more than a place to go to for a walk on a Sunday, as is shown by the many cafés and restaurants in the main street and square. After a meal here, and if the weather is fine, go and enjoy the superb view of Lyons from the Place de l'Eglise, where there is also an orientation table, and then visit the Maison de l'Araire, which exhibits this society's research on the history and traditions of the Lyonnais region. The megaliths of the Bois du Fay and Col du Colombier are worth visiting, as is the Romanesque chapel of Châteauvieux, which is reached by way of the surfaced road beyond the Carmelite monastery, unless you prefer to go rock-climbing up to the top of Py-Froid or to take a pedalo or go fishing on Lac Ronzey (an anagram of Yzeron). You can return to Lyons by the D 122 through Saint-Martin-en-Haut, a large village which is the location each year for the 'Foire des Monts du Lyonnais' at the end of September. The hamlet of Rochefort, which is 1.5 kilometres from Saint-Martin, was annexed to its neighbour in 1814, and looks as though it is frozen in

*The monastery was built
between 1956 and 1959 in
shuttered concrete.*

*Yzeron has become a favourite
spot for Sunday walks.*

*The Etang du Ronzey (an anagram of Yzeron)
has both pedalos and fishing.*

time with its ruined keep and walls, houses with carved or emblazoned lintels, a 12th and 16th century chapel with a 'pieta' (the Virgin Mary holding the dead body of Christ on her lap or in her arms) in polychrome stone, a beautiful altarpiece, and a 12th century stained glass window. This region was very hostile to the French Revolution, and it was here that was formed a band of brigands called the 'Chauffeurs du Lyonnais' who used to 'chauffer' (heat up) their victims' feet to make them confess where their money was hidden. On the D 11 lies Thurins, the raspberry and soft fruits capital, where the fruit festival takes place on the second Sunday in September. At Brindas, a name that for a long time was synonymous for the people of

Lyons with 'back of beyond' ('Tu viens bien de Brindas' – 'You really do come from the back of beyond'), turn right onto the D 50 to reach, on the other side of the village of Chaponost in the Plat de l'Air area, the Arches of Chaponost. These 72 arches in a remarkably good state of preservation are important remains of the Gier aqueduct, which was one of four aqueducts that used to supply water to Roman Lyons.

The 'route des crêtes' (route of the mountain crests) is a variation of this second itinerary. It starts after Craponne, when, after going through Grézieu-la-Varenne, the D 24 rises up to the Col de la Luère (714 metres), a starting-point for several walks. In 1922, Mère Brazier opened a restaurant here, and its food and wine were duly awarded 3 stars by the Michelin guide, a fact that had a good number of the celebrities of the time, including General de Gaulle and the Aga Khan, beating a track to the area. Continue on the D 113 to Saint-Bonnet-le-Froid where a neo-feudal château stands among box trees and clipped yews, pine trees, and terraces. This is the ideal place to have tea and admire the countryside, which stretches out as far as the eye can see to the Beaujolais and the Alps. It gets its name from the fact that the people of Clermont-Ferrand stopped there in 722 to look for the body of their bishop, St Bonnet, who had died at Lyons 12 years previously. The chapel, which underwent alterations in 1844, dates from the 8th century and is a place of pilgrimage. Continue on the same route to arrive at the Col de Malval, another starting-point for walks, where you can stop for lunch. Go down the D 50 to Courzieu, a very old village that stands on the Roman road to Aquitaine, of which several old 15th century houses which used to be as inns are a reminder. The tradition here of strawberry growing has given rise to an annual strawberry festival, but it is, however, the animal park half-way between Malval and Courzieu that has made the village so well-known today. The park, whose timber and earthen buildings are of Scandinavian inspiration, extends over a 20-hectare site. Its primary attractions are demonstrations, with commentary, of birds of prey in free flight, and also a forest discovery trail which enables the observation of the birds of prey in their cages, as well as that of a variety of European animals, including predators, in addition to flowers, trees, and the world of bees. Take the N 496 to get back to Lyons by the D 7 or the N 7.

The Monts du Lyonnais.

Yzeron stands perched on a rock.

THE SAÔNE VALLEY
AND THE MONTS-D'OR

This trip is also a favourite with the people of Lyons, and is takes in two complementary destinations, the Saône plain and the limestone hills of the Monts-d'Or, which form part of the same layer of sedimentary rocks that used to cover the Massif Central. Ever since Roman times, Lyons has made full use of the springs that emerge at the foot of their slopes, and since the Middle Ages, quarries have been dug into the grey or ochre-coloured limestone in order to extract stone for the construction of houses in the city. From the 17th century, the wealthier of Lyons' residents built their summer country residences here, and although many have now disappeared, this residential aspect of the area has lasted right up to the present day. You can follow the river, climb up into the Monts-d'Or, or do a mixture of both.

Access to the Saône Valley is either by Caluire or by following the river from the exit of the Croix-Rousse tunnel. The first route has the advantage of passing an important Resistance site, as it was at Caliure that Jean Moulin was arrested during a meeting with Dr Dugoujon. The house, now a listed building, is still there, at the top of the Montée Castellane, and a memorial to the event stands in the Rue Jean Moulin. On the way down the Montée Castellane, there is beautiful view of the Île Barbe and its abbey ruins.

The second route passes some lovely 18th and 19th century houses along the Quai Clemenceau, as well as, at the bottom of the Montée des Forts, the Château de Cuire-les-Bas and the Maison de la Rivette, which was built by Soufflot in a very classical style, and which stands above an Italian-style terraced garden. This beautiful bourgeois house is occupied today by a multilingual school.

After the Île Roy, the Quai Jean-Baptiste Simon runs alongside the village of Fontaines-sur-Saône, the birthplace

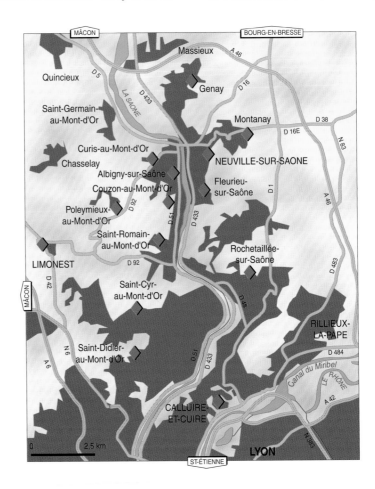

of Joseph Sève, who achieved fame in Egypt under the name of Suliman Pasha. Continue on the right bank to reach Rochetaillée-sur-Saône, which is an attractive hilltop village that used to be a favourite bathing place for the people of Lyons, and which today is popular with vintage car enthusiasts. The village's 12th to 15th century (with 19th century alterations) château houses the Musée Henri Malartre, where bicycles, motorbikes, trams, and cars are displayed, thereby demonstrating the evolution of these means of transport. Specific individual exhibits can also be examined, such as Edith Piaf's Packard, the American cars of France's favourite comedian, Coluche, and of the Champagne magnate, Monsieur Pommery, as well as Adolf Hitler's armoured Mercedes.

The route then passes through Fleurieu-sur-Saône, where, in factories that can still be seen today, J.-B. Guimet invented 'Guimet blue', an artificial ultramarine blue that revolutionised the dyeing industry. The small neighbouring town of Neuville gets its name from the Archbishop of Lyons, Camille de Neuville, who was an extremely important figure in the city between 1653 and 1693, and who built his hunting residence here. Not much remains of his château of Ombreval, which is now the town hall, but there are lovely views of the Saône from the gardens, in which is a beautiful grotto. The edge of the town centre is marked by streets that follow the line of the old walls, and the 12th century church has an attractive Rococo interior. Take the D 16 from Neuville to Montanay, which has a small Romanesque church with wall-

paintings, and from where a superb view of the Saône Valley can be enjoyed. Go back down and carry on to the village of Genay, which still has its 15th century 'poype', a fortification that is characteristic of the Bresse region.

Take the right bank of the river back

The evolution of car design and construction can be followed at the museum.

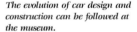

The Henri Malartre car museum is housed in the château of Rochetaillée-sur-Saône.

The gardens of the château of Ombreval in Neuville contain a magnificent grotto.

The château of Ombreval in Neuville (the present town hall).

to Lyons, crossing the Saône by the bridge at Neuville. All along the D 433 lie villages which make the most of their situation, with landing stages for activities on the river, 'guinguettes' (open-air cafés or restaurants with dance-floors), which serve 'friture' (fried small river fish) and 'fromage blanc à la crème', and shady corners where 'boules' can be played. Moreover, at Albigny-sur-Saône is a 12th century keep, a large house where the frescoes painted by Daniel Sarrabat in 1710 have recently been restored, and a 100-year old gingko biloba tree, around which has been constructed the school dedicated to the Voisin brothers, who were aviation pioneers who lived here at Couzon, where Jacquard, the inventor of the mechanical loom, spent his childhood. There is also the 19th century church built by Bossan, the architect of church at Fourvière, the 13th century frescoes of the Château de la Guerrière, the remains of the 1993 landslide, the lock, and a river museum which is housed in an old barge.

Starting the visit to the Monts-d'Or at France's most famous restaurant, that of Paul Bocuse at Collonges, may be an excellent introduction to the subject, but it is not within everybody's reach. Ten or so villages stand on the slopes of Mont Verdun (625 m), Mont Thou (609 m), and Mont Cindre (469 m). Access to them by the eastern side is by the many small roads that come off the D 51, or by the western side by the minor roads that come off the D 42, or by the centre, from the Monts-d'Or crossroads at Vaise. Waymarked footpaths leave from Albigny, Couzon, and Curis. The area's main attraction is the number of beautiful

views that it offers. There are some old ruins, most notably the Mont-d'Or aqueduct, châteaux from different periods, medieval churches, and 'cabornes' (stone cabins with conical roofs which provided shelter for shepherds).

If the area is entered from the south by way of Vaise, the first place you come to is Saint-Cyr-au-Mont-d'Or, an old village which is dominated by the old château keep, and where the church tower has been converted into a multi-purpose hall. The partly medieval Château de Fromente stands in the next village of Saint-Didier-au-Mont-d'Or. Take the D 73 to Saint-Fortunat, whose cha-

The sundial on the front of the restaurant.

The entrance to Paul Bocuse's restaurant.

pel has a Gothic nave, and which also has some old stone quarries. Wide, sweeping views in every direction can be enjoyed from Mont Thon, from where the Monts du Lyonnais to the west, Lyons to the south, Poleymieux to the north, and the Saône, the Jura, and the Alps to the east can all be seen. Go back down to Saint-Romain-au-Mont-d'Or, 'the pearl of the Monts d'Or', which has a wealth of historical features, such as the Roman aqueduct, the 15th century Château de la Bessée, the private La Fretta gardens, which were laid out by Soufflot between 1759 and 1766 for the botanist, P. Poivre, and the church with its Romanesque apse, two side chapels, a 15th century stained glass window, and an 18th century nave. Inside is a holy water stoup for

Couzon's church was built in the 19th century by Bossan, who also designed the church at Fourvière.

children that has been added to the adults' stoup, with two other stoups, from the 17th and 18th centuries, on the outside the church. Take the D 89 to Curis, which has old houses built of golden stone, the 12th, 13th, and 18th century château that was constructed on the site of an old Roman fort, and the aqueduct in the La Trolanderie part of the village. Take the D 73 to Poley-mieux-au-Mont-d'Or, a village founded in Roman times, which has many old houses built in the local golden stone, examples of which are the Maison du Barbier and the Tour Risler, which is all that remains of the 12th century château. The 'Halle Paysanne' (Farmers' Hall) is the market-place for the products, especially goat's cheeses, of what is a primarily an agricultural region.

THE BEAUJOLAIS

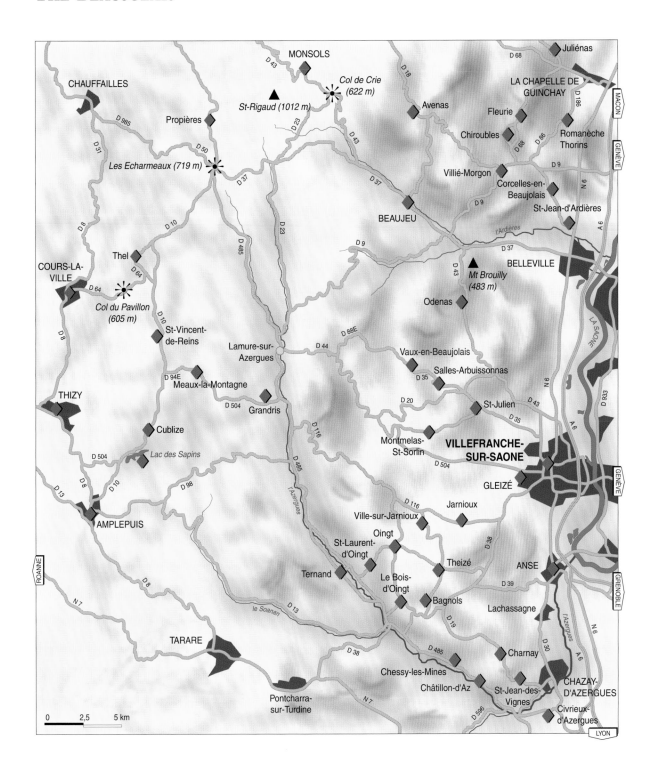

*Saint-Jean-des-Vignes
has a quarry which has been
turned into a regional
geology centre.*

Ampère's house, which was purchased
and restored by the American Behn
brothers, was converted into a museum
of electricity in 1931. Enjoy the beautiful views from Croix Rampeau, and
then take the D 42 to Mont Verdun,

*The old feudal château
of Charnay.*

116

which is dominated by the radar equipment on the air base that controls all the airspace in south-east France, and of which part of the installations and anti-nuclear shelters excavated deep into the rock emerges at the surface. Next, overlooked by the 17th century Château de la Barollière, comes the village of Limonest, which was an old staging-post on the royal road to Paris, a fact borne out by its two old inns. Return to Lyons by Champagne-au-Mont-d'Or.

THE BEAUJOLAIS

With its hills and valleys, its churches and châteaux, its cellars for wine-tasting and museums, the Beaujolais is a practically inexhaustible source of visits and walks all by itself. This route, which is of a necessity far too

Châtillon-d'Azergues is built on a rocky spur.

short, goes through this beautiful region's major places of interest, which should be explored at a leisurely pace and also throughout the different seasons, as the vines' changing colours of green, golden brown, and red give the countryside a different sort of atmosphere every time.

MAIRIE

117

*The 11th and 15th century
fortified château hangs
over the Azergues valley.*

THE AZERGUES VALLEY

This is the country of the 'golden stones', that golden or reddish-tinted limestone whose colour also changes according to the light and the seasons. It is plentiful in the Beaujolais, where it used to be used a great deal in the construction of villages, churches, and châteaux. Most of the quarries are closed today, but the Azergues Valley has pre-served this goldenness of colour which stands out to such good effect in the countryside, which, with its valleys and hillside fortresses, is often compared to that of Tuscany. Leave Lyons by the N 6, then take the D 485 in the direction of Civrieux-d'Azergues and Lausanne, before turning right onto the D 30 to Saint-Jean-des-Vignes, which has converted its old quarry into an 'Espace Pierres Folles' (Mad Stones Centre),

Street entertainment in Oingt.

Bagnols' 15th century crenellated château is now a member of the 'Relais et Châteaux' hotel association

which describes the area's geological history. After that, make time for a leisurely visit of the thirty golden-stone villages.

At Charnay, the old feudal château that was rebuilt in the 17th century now houses the 'mairie', and a beautiful 13th century St Christopher in polychrome stone stands imposingly in the church. In Chatillon-d'Azergues, which is built on a rocky spur, its 11th and 15th century fortified château, overlooking the Azergues Valley, is very impres-

Beaujeu was the old capital of the Beaujolais until the 15th century. Its church of Notre-Dame-des-Marais is worth a visit.

sive when seen from the road and from the village. (The château is open to visitors on the 'Journées du Patrimoine' in September). The old Romanesque chapel nearby is open on Sunday afternoons from Easter to All Saints' Day.

After Chessy-les-Mines, with its beautiful church and its 16th century 'Jacques Coeur' window, turn right onto the D 19 to Bagnols, where the 15th century château surrounded by crenellated walls is today the home of a 'Relais et Châteaux' luxury hotel. To then get to Oingt, take either the direct route on the D 120 or make a short detour through Le Bois-d'Oingt, Ternard, both of which are

fortified villages, and then Saint-Laurent-d'Oingt. Listed as an historical monument since 1947, Oingt still has the arched gateway of its old walls, and beautiful narrow medieval streets with typical names like, 'Trayne-cul' (of which 'laggard' is a possible, polite translation) or 'Coupe-jarret' (cutthroat), which climb up to the church, from where there are superb views. Théizé must be visited to see the lovely Château de Rochebonne, then Ville-sur-Jarnioux and Jarnioux, whose fine multi-towered château can only be visited from the outside, before reaching Villefranche-sur-Saône. This is the present capital of the

The château of Montmelas-Saint-Sorlin with its round towers.

Beaujolais, having ousted Beaujeu from the position during the 15th century. Its church of Notre-Dame-des-Marais and its many Renaissance houses on the Rue Nationale make it worth a long visit. On the last Sunday in January each year, the town welcomes the 'Vague', which is a festival for conscripts, who wear dinner suits and top hats for the occasion. Finally, a last detour has to be made by the N 6 to visit Anse. This small hilltop town had been settled by the Celts and the Romans, from which latter period there is a mosaic displayed at the château, before it became one of the gateways to the Lyonnais region. Its medie-

Villefranche-sur-Saône.

Villefranche-sur-Saône's church.

The Musée Claude Bernard, named after the founder of experimental medicine.

A portrait of Claude Bernard.

val past is illustrated by the Château des Tours, which was built in the 13th century by the canon-counts of Lyons.

THE SLOPES
OF THE BEAUJOLAIS

Fleurie, Chirouble, Villié-Morgon, Juliénas... so many names with which to excite the palates of wine connoisseurs. Before setting off to explore this wine-growing part of Beaujolais, here are two statistics : there are 22,500 hectares of vineyards in the Beaujolais, and 170 million bottles of wine are produced every

Wine cellars at the château of La Chaize.

year. From Villefranche-sur-Saône, take the D 504 in the direction of Gleizé, and then Montmelas-Saint-Sorlin, where, just like in a child's drawing, the medieval château has tall, round towers topped with pointed roofs, and where the French-style formal gardens and wine-tasting in the cellar are additional attractions. Take the D 44 to Saint-Julienas-en-Beaujolais, where the Musée Claude Bernard is to be found in the house of the French physiologist and founder of modern experimental medicine. In Salles-Arbuissonais, the priory's cloisters and Romanesque church, as well as the houses in the Place du Chapitre, which are somewhat later in date, make up a beautiful architectural group, which was founded in the 10th century by the powerful Cluny Abbey. After a minor detour to Vaux-en-Beaujolais, which was the setting for the novel, 'Clochemerle', by Gabriel Chevalier, take the D 43, where, at the exit to Odenas, the elegant architecture of the Château de la Chaize is reflected in a lake surrounded by formal gardens that were laid out by Lenôtre and Mansart. (The château's wine cellars and gardens can be visited by appointment). After Mont Brouilly, continue to Beaujeu. The former capital of the lords of Beaujeu was founded in the 10th century, and the reign of Anne de Beaujeu, Louis XI's daughter and regent of the kingdom of France until her death in 1483, left a great impression on it, as, for example, the Romanesque church of Saint-Nicholas owes its decoration to her. The 'Sources du Beaujolais' wine centre is housed in a 16th century half-timbered apothecary's house, and the Musée des Arts et Traditions Populaires has displays of traditional regional arts and crafts. Along the D 26, the great names of the Beaujolais vineyards are then encountered, starting with Juliénas, in the north, one of whose wine-tasting cellars is to be found in the old village church. A short detour is recommended to Romanèche-Thorens to visit the 'Hameau-en-Beaujolais' (Beaujolais hamlet), where, in the village's old station, about fifteen rooms relate the history of wine and wine-making. Afterwards, take the 'Route des Crus' (Route of the Great Wines), which runs southwards through Fleurie, Chiroubles, and Villié-Morgon. Two kilometres from Villié-Morgon lies the château of Corcelles-en-Beaujolais, which was first built in the 13th century,

Detail of the pillars in the cloister of Salles Arbuissonas Priory.

A look of Tuscany in the Beaujolais.

A view of Vaux-en-Beaujolais, the source of inspiration for Gabriel Chevalier's novel, 'Clochemerle'.

The Maison du Col de Crie.

The wine harvest.

and later rebuilt in the 15th and 16th centuries. Part of the château, including the interior courtyard, the chapel, the oubliettes, and the kitchens, as well as the wine-making vats, can be visited.

Mont Saint-Rignaud.

The last stage of the tour begins at Saint-Jean-d'Ardières, where, standing alongside the N 6, the Maison des Beaujolais has both a restaurant and a wine-tasting area, where the full range of Beaujolais wines can be enjoyed.

THE MONTS DU BEAUJOLAIS

A visit to the region would not be complete without seeing the Monts du Beaujolais, which are in the far west of the department of the Rhône, next to that of the Loire. This is where Tuscany is left behind and Canada makes its appearance, as the rugged slopes are covered with coniferous forests. This is the countryside of mushrooms and also of hiking, which is a popular pastime with the people of Lyons between spring and autumn. Two routes are possible from Lamure-sur-Azergues. The first climbs up to the Col des Echarmeaux (719 m), continues to Proprières, and then to Monsols, passing Mont Saint-Rigaud, the highest point in the Beaujolais at over 1,000 metres. At the foot of the mountain, the Maison du Col de Crie (822 m) has a keep-fit exercise trail, a picnic site, and several sporting and tourist activities. The return trip goes along the D 18 through Avenas, with its Romanesque church built in the style of Cluny. The second route follows the 'Route des Sapins' (Road of the Fir-Trees), which goes through Grandis and the Col de Cambuse, then Cublize up to the Lac des Sapins. The route then carries on to Amplepuis, the birthplace of Bartélémy Thimonnier, the inventor of the sewing machine, whose museum stands on the Place de l'Hôtel de Ville, and then continues through Thizy, the former stronghold of the lords of Beaujeu, Cours-la-Ville, the Col du Pavillon, Thel, and Saint-Vincent-de-Renneins to the beautiful village of Meaux-la-Montagne.

Countryside in Cenves-Avenas.

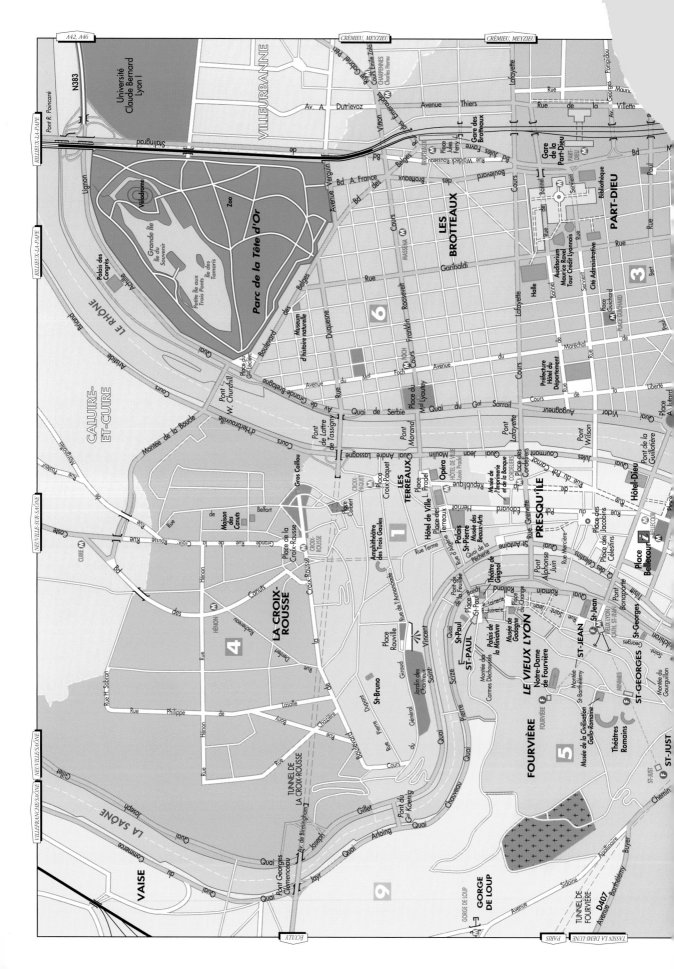

SANS-SOUCI

Cours Albert Thomas

Avenue des Frères Lumière

Vers l'Institut Lumière

L'ISLE D'ABEAU

Satolas, CHAMBÉRY
GRENOBLE

Rue Marius Berthet

Boulevard des États-Unis

Musée Urbain
Tony Garnier

Rue de l'Épargne

Merle

Rue des Tchécoslovaques

Gambetta

Combattants

Guillotière

GARIBALDI

Garibaldi

Faure

Ribaldi

Felix

Garibaldi

LA GUILLOTIÈRE

CASERNE
SERGENT BLANDAN

Rue du Pressé

Avenue

Berthelot

N7

Route de Vienne

Rue du Vivier

VIENNE

SAXE
GAMBETTA

Grande

Rue

Avenue

Marseille

Rue

Rue de l'Université

Rue Marc Bloch

Place
Jean Macé

VIEUX MACÉ

Rue Berthelot

Rue Gerland

Rue de Gerland

LA SAÔNE

Rue Claude

Pont de
l'Université

Centre d'Histoire
de la Résistance et
de la Déportation

Rue Garibaldi

Avenue

Avenue

Musée des
Arts Décoratifs

Pont
Gallieni

Quai

Musée
des Tissus

Quai

Rue

Rue

Rue

Rue Leclerc

LE RHÔNE

Avenue

Rue

d'Ainay

AMPÈRE
VICTOR HUGO

Place Carnot

Centre
d'Échanges
Perrache

Gare de
Perrache

Rue de Perrache

Quai Charlemagne

Rue Childebert

7

Rue du Mal Joffre

Pont
Kitchener
Marchand

Rue Vauban

PERRACHE

A7-E15

N446

Quai

Quai des Étroits

Quai

Rambaud

Pont de la
Mulatière

Pont Pasteur

Place
Antonin
Perrin

Grande Halle
Tony Garnier

Avenue Tony Garnier

Cours Garibaldi

Allée Pierre de Coubertin

GERLAND

Stade de
Gerland

Palais des
Sports

STE-FOY-
LÈS-LYON

Av. de la 1re Division
Française Libre

Rue du
Commandant
Charcot

FRANCHEVILLE

Quai Jean-Jacques Rousseau

Quai

D487

D486

LA MULATIÈRE

MARSEILLE, ST-ÉTIENNE

OULLINS

ST-FOYS

VIENNE

D15

500 mètres

Plan du Métro

Lyon.

A — L. BONNEVAY

Cusset

Flachet

Grotte Ciel

CHARPENNES
Charles Hernu

Masséna

République
Villeurbanne

Monplaisir
Lumière

Grange-Blanche

Loënnec

Mermoz-Pinel

Parilly

D — GARE DE VENISSIEUX

Sans-Souci

HÔTEL DE VILLE
Louis Pradel

Foch

Brotteaux
Part-Dieu

C — CUIRE

Hénon

Croix-Rousse

Croix-Paquet

Cordeliers

Pl. Guichard

Saxe-
Gambetta

Bellecour

Guillotière

Ampère-
Victor Hugo

B — JEAN MACÉ

A — PERRACHE

VIEUX-
LYON
Cath. St-Jean

Fourvière

Funiculaire

Minimes

St-Just

GORGE
DE LOUP

D

© 2001 - Édilarge SA, Éditions Ouest-France, Rennes
Cet ouvrage a été achevé d'imprimer en France par l'imprimerie Pollina (85) - n° L99581
Photogravure Nord Compo Villeneuve d'Ascq (59)
ISBN : 2.7373.2813.6 - Dépôt légal : juin 2001
N° d'éditeur : 4189.02.1,5.03.06